UNLOCKING
THE
JOB MARKET

UNLOCKING
THE
JOB MARKET

A Step-by-Step Guide
to
Successful Job Hunting

JAMES L. HAMMOND

Dunmore Publishing Company
New Bern, North Carolina

Published by Dunmore Publishing Company
P. O. Box 2411, New Bern, N.C. 28561-2411

Library of Congress Catalog Card Number: 88-83993

ISBN: 0-924519-03-7

Manufactured in the United States of America

Printed and Bound by
Griffin & Tilghman Printers, Inc.
New Bern, North Carolina,

About the Author

Extensive association with the utility and chemical industries has given James L. Hammond a comprehensive understanding of business practices and a deep insight into the corporate environment. He has held high-level management positions in several major corporations and has sat on both sides of the interviewing table. Mr. Hammond now lives in eastern North Carolina with his wife and children.

Dedication

For their love, patience and encouragement, I dedicate this book to my wife, Myra, and to my children: Cynthia, David, Elizabeth and Melissa.

Table of Contents

Acknowledgements

I want to express my sincerest gratitude to those fine people mentioned here who, while helping me to bring this book to its completion, shared my enthusiasm for it and gave me encouragement.

For critical reading of the manuscript and for their many helpful suggestions: Capt. John B. Castano, U.S. Navy (Ret.), B. Troy Ferguson, Jr., Edith H. Ferguson, Bruce Lee Gage and Frances P. Phelps. For typing the manuscript and being a constant sounding board: my wife, Myra W. Hammond.

Preface

When I set out to look for my first career job after graduating from college, I was both baffled and intimidated by the mystique and power of the men and women who sat behind large desks covered with important-looking paraphernalia and who, with not much more than a nod of the head, could either hire me or send me on my way. These people, I thought, must be direct descendants of the gods. I had to do something about my feelings of inadequacy in job interview situations, so I read books and exposed myself to some counseling on the subject. This took place over a long period of time, and, meanwhile, I continued to interview intermittently for better jobs. I was getting better at it, but not good enough. The books I was reading were somewhat frivolous and poorly organized. None of them covered the gamut of job-hunting procedures. They were incomplete. The counseling service was much better, but it left something to be desired; and it was expensive. I was in a quandary, and I decided to do something about it.

I had accumulated a great deal of knowledge about the art of job hunting: from the books I had read, the counseling I had received and, most of all, my own job-hunting experiences. I pulled it all together into a concise, well organized plan covering all the aspects and requirements of a successful job-search campaign. I began to use it, and it was amazingly effective.

Using my newly developed job-search campaign plan as a guide, I successfully changed jobs four times during my career and quickly reached the highest level of responsibility in my area of expertise, starting out as an accountant and moving up through the levels of first-line supervision and middle management to the position of Senior Vice President of a major corporation. In the meantime, I showed the plan to others and counseled them on how to use it. It proved so successful that I decided to make it available to job hunters everywhere, most of whom, including the highest-level executives, don't know how to go about finding a job.

There are a number of books which address the subject of job hunting, but to the best of my knowledge none of them are as comprehensive, yet as direct and to the point, as this one. Each expert in this field has his own variations on how a job-search campaign should be organized and conducted; and, while the differences often appear to be insignificant, they can be critical to the success of the endeavor. The principles set forth in this book have been tested and have proved to be singularly effective in generating job offers.

There are more than a few employment consultants and outplacement counselors who offer their services on a one-on-one basis to people who are active in the job market. Employment consultants will work with anyone, while outplacement counselors specialize in helping people whose employment has been terminated involuntarily. The cost, in either case, usually runs into thousands of dollars. Therefore, if ever you should happen to be fired or forced to resign from a job, try to get the employer to send you to one of the better known outplacement consulting firms in your area and pay your expenses. If you have been a loyal, productive employee, he just might feel an obligation to agree to it.

Fortunately, the principles and techniques of successful job hunting can be learned from a home-study manual such as this one. This no-nonsense book is the culmination of years of continual research, experimentation, and practical application of these principles and techniques through counseling, and, with diligent study, it will provide you with everything you need in order to find a good job in as short a time as possible.

Much of what you will find here is not new; some of it is. What makes this book stand out from others is that it is a single source of information, in concise detail, concerning everything you need to know, from beginning to end, about how to find a job.

Before reading further, it is important for you to understand my intent in the use of the personal pronouns *he, him* and *his*. Wherever they appear in this book without their feminine counterparts, they are meant to refer to both masculine and feminine gender, thus freeing the text of the otherwise sometimes cumbersome and repetitious specific designation of the sexes.

> *"There are only two ways of getting on in this world: by one's own industry, or by the weaknesses of others."*
> —Jean de La Bruyère (1645-1696)

1
Setting the Stage: An Introduction

Job hunting can be a frustrating, even traumatic, experience; especially if you are not well prepared and organized for it. Most job seekers don't know how to organize and prepare a job-search campaign, and many who have the expertise and ability to do so are just too lazy to trouble themselves with the extra work required. Human nature being as it is, it is safe to presume that many who read these very pages will be less than diligent in their attempts at learning and applying the principles and methods discussed here. Sadly to say, therefore, the majority of people who look for jobs do it haphazardly.

The consensus among experts is that, at any point in time, there are 3-4 million people in the United States looking for jobs and that 70-75 percent of these fail to get the kinds of jobs they are looking for because they don't use the right methods. That is why you, as a serious student of this book, will have a competitive edge over others who will be looking for jobs at the same time you are.

In the following pages, you will learn how to prepare a job-search campaign portfolio, how to prepare two kinds of winning resumes and what to do with them, how to get advice interviews and why they are important to your campaign, how to stay in control of an interview, how to handle difficult interview questions and salary negotiations, how to write effective letters needed at certain stages of your campaign and, last, but equally important, how to handle yourself in your new job.

Most likely, you are reading this book because you either have (1) been fired from your job, (2) resigned (voluntarily or under pressure), (3) become dissatisfied with your present job for any number of reasons, (4) completed your formal education and are about to seek your first major job in your chosen field of specialization or (5) are about to retire from military or other government service and, hence, are looking toward the establishment of a new career. Regardless of where circumstances might place you in these several categories, these chapters will provide the knowledge and the techniques you will need to obtain the best job available in the shortest period of time.

This book is directed primarily to men and women who already are into their careers and who, for one reason or another, are looking for jobs ranging from average responsibility to the highest levels of management. However, with the exception of matters pertaining to salary negotiation (Chapter 8) and certain references to previous employment, it is of equal value to young graduates starting out to find their first jobs and offers them helpful guidance toward the advancement of their careers. It also serves as an excellent guide to people leaving military or other government service to start life anew. So no matter why you are looking for a job, and no matter what kind of job you want or what the level of the position may be, this book will help you, because the principles are basically the same in all cases.

This is a book of instruction and, as such, it should be studied and not merely read. How you will fare in your job search will depend upon how earnestly and effectively you apply what you will learn here. The only guarantee I can make is that if you do not follow this program closely, then you will not land as good a job at as high a salary and in as short a time as you otherwise could.

As in any worthwhile endeavor, success in conducting a job-search campaign will be difficult unless you radiate enthusiasm, self-confidence and a positive attitude. Important to maintaining these qualities is an adequate amount of sleep, some sensible form of exercise and a well-balanced diet (in moderate portions, of course). And above all, keep busy with your job search, especially if you are out of work. Idleness at such a time breeds worry, self-pity, low self-esteem and fear, weakening the shining qualities that attract job offers.

You must be a self-starter, because on this project you are your own boss. So get up early in the morning! Force yourself to use the telephone! Write those letters!

Finally, if you have left a previous employer under questionable circumstances and are worried about how this will affect your ability to get another job, I have these words of encouragement for you: a great many job seekers in similar situations, by applying the techniques you are about to learn, have ended their search with better and higher paying jobs than they had before. So, as you move forward with your job search, always keep in mind that good things are in store for you.

> *"I have learned this at least by my experiment: that if one advances confidently in the direction of his dreams, and endeavors to live the life which he has imagined, he will meet with a success unexpected in common hours."*
>
> —Henry David Thoreau

2
What Are Your Choices?

Are you so dissatisfied with your job that you want to quit? Or have you already quit and don't have a new job to go to? Have you been fired or forced to resign? Or have you recently retired, or are you about to retire, from military or other government service and don't know what to do next? If your answer to any of these questions is yes, then you obviously must make a decision about what to do to remedy your situation.

In each of the above circumstances, there are several choices that may be available to you. Consider the following:
- You can look for a new job.
- If your savings are adequate, you can start your own business.
  Or,
- If the circumstances are right, you can begin your actual retirement earlier than planned.

Before we examine these alternatives, let's focus briefly upon your present state of affairs.

If you have been fired or otherwise forced out of your
company, the chances are that you are harboring a great deal of
anger and resentment. You probably feel vindictive; you want
to get even. And in the background, while all this is churning
inside you, you keep searching the past for a clue as to what
really brought about your downfall. Whatever reason, if any,
was given to you at the time, you are wondering if it was the
truth. Maybe it was something else; maybe it was something
more personal — something about you that you were unaware
of and that you might have changed if you had known it would
come to this. Maybe you could have prevented it from
happening. So added to your emotional turmoil are feelings of
confusion and guilt and regret, not to mention self-pity and
fear.

All of these thoughts and feelings are natural, and probably
unavoidable. It will take time to rid yourself of them, but
meanwhile you must get on with your life. So since you can't
get rid of them here and now, push them to the back of your
mind. You must have a positive attitude in order to be able to
objectively analyze the choices available to you and make a
clear decision. It will help immensely, of course, to plunge
right in and devote your full time to consideration of the steps
you need to take to move on to better things.

If you have quit your job without first having found another
one, you have made an unfortunate mistake, because it always
is more difficult to find a job when you are unemployed. It is
unusual to leave a position voluntarily without having another
one to go to, and employers look at this with suspicion. Were
you allowed to quit to spare you the onus of being fired? Was
your performance so poor that you were almost certain that
dismissal was imminent? These are the questions that your
unemployment will raise in a prospective employer's mind;
and he naturally will be wary. But don't panic. What you have
done is not irreparable, because you will learn here how to
handle such concerns.

You probably have many of the same feelings as the person who has been terminated from his position involuntarily — anger, resentment, self-pity and fear — and, like him, you must try to push them aside. Replace these negative attitudes with positive thoughts about your future.

Next, a word to you who are so unhappy in your present job that you have decided to look for another one. Of course, that isn't necessarily the only solution for you, and it may not be the best one. The grass isn't always greener on the other side of the fence. Where you are now, at least, you are familiar with your surroundings and the attitudes of the people around you. You know the system and how it works. Moving into a totally new and unfamiliar environment can be a traumatic and unnerving experience.

Look around you. Is there something you can do to make things better for yourself right where you are? Perhaps you don't fully understand the importance of your job in the overall scheme of things. Your attitude toward it and the organization might be different if you did, so take time to look into this. Also, there may be another job in your department or elsewhere in the company that would offer you greater satisfaction. If you think that may be the case, then go for it. The important thing is to look into every possibility of finding what you want where you are now employed. If, after doing this, you find yourself facing a blank wall, then by all means go out and find another job. But please, as long as you have a choice, don't leave the job you have until you have another one definitely in hand.

Finally, if you are completing a long military or other govenment career and venturing forth into private life, you are now free to make your own decisions about where to live and what to do. You have the same choices as anyone else leaving a job. You can start a new career — a job or your own business. (In either case, you may need some additional education or training, depending upon your particular field of interest.) Or, if circumstances are favorable, you may want to take your retirement and just have fun with it. Most likely, however, you will want to find something financially rewarding to do, especially if you are relatively young. In any event, the fact is that you have a choice for your future.

Now, let's take a look at early retirement. I mean *real* retirement, without making any sustained effort to earn additional income.

When, for whatever reason, you find yourself without a job or have decided to leave the one you have, retirement, as mentioned before, may be one of the several choices available to you. If your personal financial plan includes reliance upon a company or government pension, you will have to meet certain minimum age and/or length-of-service requirements in order to qualify for it. There may be other requirements. Ask your plan administrator or personnel officer what they are.

If early retirement *is* your preference, you probably will need substantial savings to supplement your pension. Otherwise, it is likely that your income will be inadequate to prevent a significant decline in your standard of living. As a matter of fact, your savings should be considerable no matter *when* you choose to retire, because even a full pension may not be sufficient to provide you with a comfortable lifestyle. After all, retirement is the time to do all those things you didn't have time to do when you were busy with your career, and if your funds are so limited as to deprive you of all recreational activity, your idleness will depress you. Even worse would be a financial position so weak that you would be unable to provide reasonable necessities for yourself and those dependent upon you. So unless your financial situation is adequate for the level of comfort you are willing to accept, don't retire until you have to.

Regardless of monetary considerations, retirement is not a state of bliss for everyone, and it may not be for you. There are those who simply cannot abide an idle moment of their waking hours. If you are one of them and have no hobbies of meaningful substance, or other strong interests unrelated to your work, you probably would find retirement to be intolerable. Therefore, early retirement would be a mistake for you.

Have you had thoughts, from time to time, about starting your own business? If you have, this is an appropriate time to seriously consider it. "Seriously" is the key word here. Don't commit yourself in any way without taking into consideration every angle. Of all new business ventures started, many more fail than succeed. The two main reasons for this are insufficient funds and lack of knowledge. So before you become too enthusiastic, be absolutely certain that you will have ready access to enough money — both from your personal savings and, as may be necessary, from borrowings — to cover the financial requirements of the business *and* your living expenses until such time as you would conservatively expect the business to generate cash adequate for these purposes. And, by all means, make certain that you have in-depth knowledge of the product or service that you intend to sell; otherwise, you will find it difficult, if not impossible, to obtain financial backing from outside sources.

If, after considering early retirement and/or starting your own business, you decide that neither of them is right for you, you are left with the final, and most likely your best, alternative: finding another job. But don't look at this as being a last resort. The very thought process that brought you to this conclusion makes it abundantly clear that it is the most suitable choice for you. So be enthusiastic and happy about it. Just think! You're going to get back on course with a career! And I'm going to help you do it.

"Do what you can, with what you have, where you are."
                                                —Theodore Roosevelt

3

The Waiting Game: A Hit-or-Miss Approach

The only things that most people know to do when they start out to look for a job are to register with as many employment agencies as they can, read and answer the job advertisements in newspapers and scatter their resumes around to everyone they can think of. And then, thinking they have done all they can, they sit and wait for things to happen.

Certainly, you should not ignore any source where there might be even a remote possibility of obtaining a job interview; but you should be aware of the effectiveness of each source. Obviously, some are better than others.

EMPLOYMENT AGENCIES

Don't overlook the broad category of employment agencies, but at the same time don't relax and rely solely upon them. For the most part, they are not working for you.

Within this classification are the so-called "flesh peddlers", who get their employment listings primarily from job advertisements in newspapers. Basically, all they do is send you to an employer to fill out an employment application and leave you to fend for yourself. Their main concern is to find a body for a job. It doesn't matter to them who it is. They deal with jobs paying up to about $25,000 per year, and you will pay them a fee, if you are hired, based upon the starting salary.

Next in this category are the placement agencies, which maintain contact with employers to keep abreast of their personnel requirements. These agencies do some screening of candidates to assure that there is a good match for the employer's needs. Nevertheless, they tend to use the "shotgun" method: sending people, one after another, to employment interviews with the hope that, statistically, one of them will get the job. These agencies generally focus their attention on jobs paying from $25,000 to $50,000 a year, and in many cases the placement fee is paid by the employer.

Finally, there are the executive search firms, commonly referred to as "headhunters". These usually are very prestigious firms, located in metropolitan centers, who work on behalf of employers all over the country and, in fact, throughout the world. The employer pays the search firm a retainer to find the right person for the job. A consultant at the firm meets with the employer to learn as much as possible about the company and the requirements of the position to be filled. Then the search firm goes through a very thorough process of screening prospective candidates before making its recommendations to the employer, and from these recommendations the employer decides which candidates he wishes to interview.

While it does no harm to let search firms know that you would like to be considered for a job, they have their own preferred methods of locating people. There is a consensus among executive search consultants that people who are not actively seeking a career change make the best candidates to bring to an employer's attention. Therefore, search firms tend to make job hunters out of people who otherwise would not be considering a change in employment. What usually happens is that the search consultant calls a currently employed individual, whose name has been extracted from any one of a number of published directories, explains to him the job requirements and responsibilities and asks if he could suggest someone who might be interested in the position. The actual intent is to give the called party an opportunity to name himself as a possible candidate.

When dealing with an executive search firm, no fees or expenses are incurred by any of the candidates, whether successfully placed or not, since all costs, including those related to attending interviews, generally are paid by the employers represented by the search firm. Jobs handled by search firms are high-level positions paying in excess of $50,000 to as much as $200,000 annually or more.

NEWSPAPER ADVERTISEMENTS

Your job-search campaign plan also should include keeping abreast of jobs advertised in the classified pages of newspapers. However, you should realize that this is a very low-yield source of job possibilities. Oftentimes, such advertisements describe jobs which do not even exist, serving, rather, as a vehicle for public relations or institutional advertising. However, this is not generally the case with regard to ads placed in military or government-service trade journals. Such ads usually are bona fide representations of real job opportunities.

Employment agencies often place blind ads (in which advertisers are not identified) to build up their resume files. On the other hand, a blind ad could be one placed by your own company — there is no sure way of knowing — so you should be careful about responding to such advertisements.

Job advertisements in *The Wall Street Journal, The New York*

Times and other major newspapers receive literally hundreds of responses. That makes for a lot of competition, and the odds in favor of your getting an interview are very poor — almost infinitesimal, in fact. In many instances, you will not even receive an acknowledgement to your response, particularly where blind ads are concerned. Nevertheless, you should not ignore newspaper advertisements, because there is at least a remote chance that a bona fide job contact might be made, and you don't want to miss that possibility.

In order to get any attention at all, your response to a job advertisement must stand out from all other responses and convince the reader that you meet all the requirements of the job. Prior to preparing a response, read the ad carefully and underline each requirement. If you find that you do not fit all the requirements very closely, don't waste your time answering the ad. If, however, you do meet all of the requirements, prepare a letter as simply and as directly as you can.

In the first paragraph, identify with the ad by stating the title of the position and where you saw the ad.

In the second paragraph, stress how your education, experience and qualifications match the requirements of the job. If possible, use an outline form in providing this information so that it will capture the reader's attention with ease.

Finish the letter with a statement to the effect that, since you seem to meet the job requirements so well, you would like to have an opportunity to elaborate on your qualifications and background in person.

An example of an ad-response letter is shown in Appendix B.

Whether the ad does or does not request a resume — and most do — don't send one. (We will discuss in Chapter 5 how to use your resume effectively.) In some instances, a resume might give the recipient an impression that you are overqualified for the job; in others, it could give him a basis upon which to estimate your age, which, depending upon the circumstances, might also raise a problem for you. Therefore, if a resume is requested, the second paragraph of the sample letter shown in the appendix should be modified to read as follows:

> "Since I have not actively been seeking employment, I have no prepared resume, so I have listed below the indicated requirements of the position and my qualifications as they relate to them."

Likewise, if the ad asks for your salary history or your salary requirement, don't reveal it. Doing so could lead to a conclusion that you are either overqualified for the job or that you are too high-priced for the company. Therefore, if salary information is requested in the ad, insert a paragraph similar to the following between the second and third paragraphs:

> "With regard to your request for my salary history [or salary requirement], I feel that, for the present, we both are concerned mainly with determining whether or not we are a good match, after which the salary question can be easily settled. With this in mind, I would prefer to regard this matter as a subject for negotiation, and I hope you will view this approach with favor."

Before you send the letter, make several copies of it. Wait a few days and then mail another copy, attaching a note with a brief message to the effect that it is a copy of a letter which you sent several days ago and that you are following up because you feel confident that you fit the requirements of the job.

If the advertisement mentions the name of the company, there is an indirect way that you could answer it. Forget the letter. Instead, refer to the Dun & Bradstreet, Moody's, and other directories in your public library to find out whom in the organization you should contact about the ad, and call to request an interview for advice on your job-search campaign.

Don't mention the advertisement. Act as though you are not even aware of its existence. If you are so fortunate as to get an interview, even then don't acknowledge an awareness of the ad. Simply follow the procedures outlined in Chapter 6 for handling an advice interview. More than likely, the interviewer at some point will mention the advertised job, especially if he thinks you have the qualifications to match the job requirements. In this event, the advice interview will turn into a job interview.

There is a third way of answering an ad, and, again, this is possible only if you know the name of the company and whom to contact. Don't send a letter. Instead, bluff your way by telephoning a few days after the ad has appeared, claiming that you sent a letter in reply to the ad and asking to arrange a time to meet for a discussion of the job requirements and your qualifications. Although they will not be able to find a letter from you, you may get an interview.

Since your chances of getting an interview for an advertised job are so low, I suggest that you vary your approach to such ads by utilizing all three methods: the letter, solicitation of an advice interview, and the "bluff". You have nothing to lose and a slim chance of winning; and, if you are very eager for a job, even the barest chance of winning is worth the effort.

Before we leave the subject of newspaper advertisements, something should be said about job-wanted ads. These are advertisements placed by job hunters hoping to attract inquiries from employers. In a word, don't waste your time or money on them. What you will get will be phone calls and form letters from employment agencies who respond to such ads only to get resumes to add to their already bursting files.

RESUMES

The preparation and effective use of resumes is covered thoroughly in Chapter 5. For now, however, it is important for you to realize that mass distribution of resumes, a tactic used by many job hunters, is a very low producer of job interviews. In most cases, an employer's reading of a resume pertaining to someone he has never even met will raise more negative reactions than positive ones. In fact, 75 percent of all resumes received by potential employers are discarded by them without reply. So, do nothing with your resume — don't even try to write one — until you read Chapter 5.

"Even if you're on the right track, you'll get run over if you just sit there."

—Will Rogers

4

Getting There from Here:
Your Campaign Plan

People! People! People! That's how you are going to find your next job — by contacting people. Talk to everyone you know or know of, and, through them, make contacts with people *they* know. This is called networking, and the basis of it is the so-called advice interview.

At any point in time, 60-80 percent of all jobs available are unadvertised. In some cases, they are barely at the discussion stage and are merely being considered by only a few executives behind closed doors; in others, they are still in the formative stage in the deeper recesses of someone's mind, waiting to materialize. These are the people you want to reach, and the only effective way to do so is through networking and the advice interview.

ORGANIZING AND GETTING STARTED

First, you must develop a plan — a road map, if you will — to keep you from wandering about aimlessly in your search. The

31

best way to accomplish this is to go through the following
check list:

1. What is the general field of activity with which you
   wish to be associated?
      This could be business, industry, government,
      education, medical care, etc.
2. What size and type of organization do you wish to
   work for?
      Small, medium-sized or large, as defined by
      some standard, such as revenue or sales, size of
      the budget, number of customers or size of the
      geographical area served. Do you prefer a
      service organization (such as food services,
      financial services, a hotel or a hospital), a retail
      establishment, a manufacturing company, a
      commercial bank or a university?
3. What general job title and reporting level are you
   seeking?
      An example would be: "Director of Advertising.
      Reports to the Vice President of Marketing".

(Your responses to questions 1, 2, and 3 above will be
influenced largely by your previous work experience.)

4. What would be the level and job title of the person
   having authority to hire you?
      This could be more than one person. For
      example, a vice president of a company might
      be hired by the Chief Executive Officer, Chair-
      man of the Board, Executive Vice President or
      Senior Vice President.
5. Do you have a geographical preference?
      You may have a decided preference as to where
      you want to live and work; or it may be
      immaterial to you, provided the life style and
      job are satisfactory.
6. List your interviewing priorities in order of their

potential yield. (Identify all possible sources of interviews, such as primary and secondary advice and referral lists, employment agencies, newspaper advertisements, companies to be approached directly, government agencies, etc.)

For example:

(a) Primary contacts for advice and referrals. (These would be those people easiest to see.)

(b) Secondary contacts for advice and referrals. (These would be those next easiest to see.)

(c) Selected list of companies to be approached directly.

(d) Referrals from (a), (b) and (c) above.

(e) Newspaper advertisements.

(f) Employment agencies and/or search firms.

(Of course, you will approach the above sources in parallel, not sequentially.)

Now that you have outlined your campaign plan, the first step toward implementing it is to make a list of names of people you should contact. Begin by listing the names of people you would like to use as references. Get their permission to use their names and ask to meet with them to get their advice on your plan and your approach to it. Be sure to ask for suggestions as to whom else you might contact for advice.

Next, make a list of names of people who you believe would have an interest in helping you. These would include people who have a genuine concern for you, those who might feel an obligation from the past to help you and those who would help you so that you might later feel obligated to do something to benefit them. Don't overlook anyone, no matter what their station in life. To help you get started, here is a checklist of categories and sources:

- Christmas card lists
- Relatives

- Friends
- People in public life
- Clergymen
- Bankers
- Real estate brokers, insurance agents, stockbrokers
- Professional people — doctors, dentists, lawyers, accountants
- Management consultants
- Executive salesmen
- Business directories
- Organizations — professional, trade, civic, service, fraternal, etc.
- University placement departments
- Alumni associations
- Church-affiliated organizations
- Chamber of Commerce
- Telephone book "yellow pages"

These will be your contacts and/or sources for advice and referrals. After you have completed the list, break it down into two parts — primary contacts (those who will be easiest to see) and secondary contacts (those next easiest to see). Spend a lot of time on this list, because it is the backbone of your campaign. Don't prejudge anyone. The most menially employed person you know may have some very high-level connections.

Having completed your list of names, you then should begin to contact each individual by telephone or by letter, depending upon how well you know him or her, explaining what you are involved in and asking for an interview for advice. If your initial contact is by letter, it should be followed with a telephone call for the specific purpose of arranging a time and place for a meeting. In either event, make it clear that you are not asking, and will not ask, for a job. (In Chapter 9 we will discuss in detail how to prepare a letter requesting an advice interview.)

Next, prepare a list of companies which interest you and the names of their senior officers and department heads. But avoid personnel managers. They usually are not familiar with all the needs of other departments and lack authority to hire. Make your contacts with people who have functional authority over the area of your interest.

After sending a letter to introduce yourself and explain your mission, you will solicit advice interviews from companies in your area by telephone. As for distantly located companies, send a letter to let them know that you are available in the job market. (Chapter 9 includes a thorough discussion of how to prepare a letter of availability.) You can find these companies, along with their addresses and the names of their principal officers and managers, listed in Moody's industrial and public utility manuals, *Dun & Bradstreet's Million Dollar Directory, Standard and Poor's Register of Corporations, Directors and Executives* and various other business directories. Most public libraries have these reference sources.

Don't lose sight of your objectives during an advice interview. Getting advice is not your real objective, even though you said it was when you asked for the interview. It is to get a job offer. Your alternative objective is to get referrals to expand your network for more interviews. If advice should be all you get, however, the interview has been worth the effort, because even the least bit of information could point you in a direction that might lead you to a job opportunity.

Keep a list of referrals, and, whenever you get new ones, add the names to the list. Then contact them just as you have others. Those nearby will be contacted for advice interviews, and those at some distance will be made aware of your availability.

Be sure to understand that you are not asking for advice interviews when you write to distantly located companies. The cost of overnight accomodations, meals and air fare is too much to incur for a mere fishing expedition. In your letters of availability, you must make no secret of the fact that what you want is a job interview.

After mailing a batch of letters to faraway companies, and when sufficient time has elapsed to receive their replies, follow up with a telephone call to those who have not responded. Ask if your letter was received, and, if the answer is in the affirmative, say that you are calling to find out what reaction, if any, your letter may have prompted. If there appears to be no recollection of your letter, briefly recite its contents and be alert to the responses you receive. Make notes of these conversations.

After you have completed your follow-up telephone calls, go back and review the written responses you have received and the notes from your telephone conversations. If you are invited to go for an interview, by all means accept and proceed with the arrangements. The company probably will pay your expenses, in which case they will tell you so. On the other hand, you may not receive a direct invitation to an interview, but one or more of the responses may indicate more than just a passing interest in you. For instance, someone might indicate that consideration is being given to the creation of a new position, or that a vacancy is expected to occur soon, and that he will be in contact with you later. If you receive any responses of this nature, look at your financial situation to see if you can afford to make a trip to visit one or more of these companies, because a face-to-face meeting could very well be all that it would take to precipitate a decision on a job possibility. If you find that you can reasonably afford it, you should arrange meetings with as many companies as you can from whom you have had favorable responses. The way to do this is to call the companies and, after identifying yourself, say that you plan to be in their area at such and such a time and that you would like to have an opportunity to meet with them briefly while you are there. Give a time period of at least several days from which to select a meeting date in order to allow flexibility in scheduling. If more than one company is involved, arrange your itinerary in the most logical sequence that you can, consistent, of course, with the availability of the people you will be meeting.

When you arrive for your meeting, the best way to start, after introducing yourself, is by expressing your appreciation for the opportunity to meet while you are in the area and asking if there are any further thoughts or developments concerning the job possibility that was mentioned earlier. The chances are good, under the circumstances as they have developed, that the meeting will turn into a job interview. But be careful not to drop the pretense that the real purpose of your being in the area was for some reason other than to get a job interview with the company.

There are three basic rules to keep in mind as you approach your job-search campaign:

1. Be sure that your career objectives are attainable. Do not overreach your capabilities. Be realistic as to the level of the position you seek.
2. Never ask for a job when you are actively looking for one. Just let people know that you are available. If someone wants to help you but has no job available himself, asking him for one will make him feel uncomfortable, and he will want to extricate himself as quickly as possible.
3. Do not allow anyone to contact third parties on your behalf unless it is to arrange introductions for you. Insist upon doing your own talking. You are selling a product — yourself — and you know more about that product than anyone else.

THE PORTFOLIO

Just as a professional model or commercial artist carries a portfolio showing examples of his or her work, it would be helpful to you to have a portfolio of sorts when you are having your advice interviews. By bringing to the interviewer's attention certain highlights of your career, the portfolio adds credibility to any discussion of your accomplishments and capabilities.

You have a wide choice of items to include in your portfolio, such as:

- Letters of commendation.
- Newspaper or magazine articles in which you are quoted or favorably mentioned.
- Charts, graphs or tables showing results of your work.
- Awards and certificates of accomplishment.
- Photographs of impressive events involving you.
- Title pages of anything you have published.
- Programs of events where you have made presentations.
- List of names of contacts for advice interviews.
- Copy of your resume.
- Anything else of major importance relating to your present and/or previous jobs.

After you have assembled the information you plan to include in your portfolio, obtain a supply of clear plastic page-protectors punched for a three-ring binder. Insert the material in the page protectors and arrange them in the order in which you plan to talk about them. Then fasten them into a three-ring or Accopress binder.

Now you have a prop to help you through your advice interview. It gives you something visual to talk about. You might introduce it by saying, "Just to reinforce my credibility, here are a few concrete examples of some of the things I have done [holding the portfolio before the interviewer and turning the pages slowly]; and here are the names of the companies I plan to contact in this area. Do you know of anyone I should talk to at any of these companies? Can you think of any companies I should add to my list?" You have broken the ice; you both are comfortable, and you are off and running with a smooth-flowing interview.

YOUR CONTROL SYSTEM

In your job search you will be visiting a lot of places of business, talking to a lot of people and writing a lot of letters. Before long, you will be in a state of chaos unless you organize yourself at the very outset.

Use a *month-at-a-glance* calendar for scheduling interviews and other appointments and activities. Keep a history file for each person you contact. For a good filing system, use an expandable folder with alphabetically designated compartments. You may need more than one such folder, and you may have to affix the alphabetical tabs yourself. Keep a copy of all letters you send out, make notes on them when you make follow-up calls and keep them filed in your expandable folder. Also, keep a file for notes that you make in connection with interviews and telephone conversations.

"Our plans miscarry because they have no aim. When a man does not know what harbor he is making for, no wind is the right wind."

—Seneca (4 B.C. - A.D. 65)

5

The How-to's and What-for's of Resumes

Your resume is a tool to help you to convince a prospective employer to hire you and to pay you a good salary. Therefore, sufficient time should be devoted to its preparation to assure that it gives the reader the most favorable impression of you as is possible.

Your resume should state what you have done and how well you have done it and should include information regarding your work history, education, military experience, memberships and personal data. It serves as an outline for you to follow while interviewing and can provide a written summary of the interview to be left with or sent to the interviewer if so desired.

Whenever you place a resume in the mail (which, except as an accompaniment to letters of availability [see Chapter 9], is not normally recommended), be sure to enclose with it a brief and carefully prepared cover letter.

Most people are not aware of the fact that there are two types of resumes. One is the familiar chronological resume, which emphasizes your job history. The other, not so familiar, is the functional resume, which stresses your personality strengths as they relate to the work environment.

THE CHRONOLOGICAL RESUME

This is the form of resume that employment agencies and personnel departments like to see because they are accustomed to it and, therefore, are comfortable with it. An example of a chronological resume is shown in Appendix A, to which you should refer during the following explanation.

At the top of the first page of the resume, your name should appear in capital letters, followed by your home address and telephone number. The body of the resume should be organized in the following sequence:

Job Objective — Show a specific job title for the position you are seeking and, if necessary for clarification, a concise but detailed job description. Or, if you want flexibility, give a general category, such as: "Financial management position", "Production management position" or "Sales position", etc.

Job History — This should be arranged in reverse chronological order. Give the names of the companies you have worked for, the job title of each position held, and major responsibilities and achieved results in each position. Dates should not be given (more about this later).

Under major responsibilities, be sure to include those that would be most likely to impress a prospective employer.

Education — For each institution attended, first indicate the degree received and then the name of the university or college which granted it. Also indicate any special academic honors received.

If you are a college graduate, don't list your high school diploma or mention any high school awards unless the awards were unusual and exemplary. However, you should include any special courses or seminars attended, such as those sponsored by the American Management Association and most institutions of higher learning.

Military — Be brief unless it would be to your advantage to elaborate. List the highest rank attained and the specific unit and military branch in which you served. However, if you were a low-level enlisted person and won no distinctions, then simply list the branch of the military in which you served.

Personal Data — This normally includes such information as your height, weight, date of birth, marital status, number of children and status of your health. However, under certain circumstances it is advisable to finesse some of these facts or to omit them entirely.

As with other dates, never state your date of birth or your age — not on your resume, or under any other circumstances, unless specifically and forthrightly asked.

If you have minor health problems that would not impair your ability to perform your job, indicate that your health is excellent. Stating that your health is good could raise needless questions, because employers are accustomed to seeing "Health excellent" on resumes. If you can manage to walk into the workplace unassisted, then don't confuse the issue with eyebrow-raising statements unless you have an ailment which would be easily detected during a routine and cursory employment physical examination. If you obviously are overweight, don't state either your height or weight in the resume.

If you are a woman with children, don't mention them. Many employers are reluctant to hire women with dependent children for fear of the occurrence of problems which might result in excessive absenteeism. On the other hand, if you state in your resume that you have children and that they are independent and self-supporting, that would give the reader a general point of reference from which to estimate your age.

Affiliations and Memberships — If you are a member of, or are affiliated with, any organizations which would enhance your value to a prospective employer, list them. Examples of such organizations are the service clubs (such as the Rotary, Kiwanis, Lions and Civitan clubs, to name a few), the Chamber of Commerce and community-oriented organizations. Also include affiliations with professional groups, such as the various associations and societies for engineers, accountants and lawyers, among others.

As with most everything else we deal with in this life, there are both advantages and disadvantages attached to the use of the chronological resume. Most people are comfortable with this type of resume because it is the kind they are accustomed to seeing. And it is easy to prepare. But for the very reason that it emphasizes your value for work similar to that which you have done in the past, it makes it difficult for you to be considered for a change to another type of work. It also emphasizes any inconsistencies or lack of progress in your career, if either of such has been the case, sometimes leading to questions concerning what you failed to accomplish and why. Keep these thoughts in mind as you prepare your chronological resume so that you may slant it, as best you can, to emphasize the strong points that stand out in your work history and de-emphasize the weaknesses.

THE FUNCTIONAL RESUME

The functional resume differs from the chronological resume in that the emphasis is focused upon the individual's capabilities rather than his experience, relating those capabilities to the functional aspects of jobs previously held by him. An example of a functional resume can be found in Appendix A.

At the top of the first page, your name, address and telephone number should be displayed in the same manner as in the chronological resume. The following information should be included in the resume in the order given:

Job Objective — State the job title of the position you are seeking and, if necessary for clarification, a definitive but brief description of the job. However, if you prefer a broader approach, give a general category, such as: "Engineering position", "Marketing management position" or "Accounting position", etc.

Summary of Qualifications — Highlight your work experience, any especially impressive academic achievements and any citations or experiences which would emphasize your qualifications for the job objective.

Functional Background Examples — List your strongest capabilities (at least four, but no more than six). They might be, for example: leadership, tough-mindedness, ingenuity, persuasiveness, initiative and foresight. For each of them, give at least two results-oriented examples of your performance at the highest level of effectiveness through use of those capabilities, illustrating, for instance, how you increased production, improved efficiency, increased revenues or reduced cost. They should be presented by first telling exactly what you did to accomplish the attained results. Then mention any obstacles that you had to overcome in order to complete the tasks; and, finally, describe the results

that you achieved, using dollars, percentages or numer-
ical comparisons as appropriate. Begin your examples
with action words, such as *instituted*, *developed*,
directed, *recommended*, *reduced*, *increased*, etc. Keep
the sentences simple and brief. Above all, be extremely
critical of what you say in this section. Do not use any
examples that are not especially impressive. It would
be better to have only four very strong examples than
to have six that might include one or more weak ones,
because one weak example may raise doubts about all
the others.

Employment History — In reverse chronological order,
list the companies you have worked for and, in like
order, list the job titles you held in each company. If it is
important to you not to name your present employer,
instead of naming the company simply refer to it as a
"major chemical company", a "billion dollar utility
company" or a "medium-sized wholesale floor-covering
company", whatever the case may be.

Education — Same as for chronological resume.

Military Experience — Same as for chronological resume.

Personal Data — Same as for chronological resume.

Affiliations and Memberships — Same as for chronological
resume.

There are a number of advantages to the use of the functional
resume. It emphasizes your strengths and focuses attention on
information that you want to highlight. It leads a prospective
employer into consideration of ways you could be used in his
organization rather than restricting you to the narrow
boundaries of a specific job title. As a matter of fact, it is the only
type of resume that will aid you in changing from one field of
work to another, because it helps a prospective employer to

understand that, even in different fields, job functions frequently are the same. This is particularly true of non-technical fields of work. The functional resume is an especially effective tool for people changing careers after years of military or other government service.

On the other hand, this type of resume often confuses and annoys people who are so accustomed to the chronological resume. Nevertheless, you can be assured that it will be thoroughly read and favorably accepted if it is well prepared. Finally, the functional resume is far more difficult to organize than the chronological resume, but it is well worth the extra effort required.

SOME OTHER TIPS ON WRITING A GOOD RESUME

Don't crowd the resume. Maximize its readability by leaving plenty of space between captions and paragraphs. Use figures, percentages and dollar amounts. They get the attention of the reader and relieve monotony, as do parentheses, quotation marks, capital letters and underlining for emphasis. Also, avoid the use of personal pronouns and keep sentence structure and language simple.

Leave all dates off your resume: date of birth and dates of employment, graduation, military service, etc. There is no point in volunteering information which might cause a prospective employer to conclude that you are still "wet behind the ears" or that you are too old to hire. Depending upon the position, some employers will be reluctant to hire you if you are very young (say, under 30) or if you are 50 years of age or older.

Limit the resume to two pages if at all possible. Concise resumes hold the attention of the reader and force the writer to focus on only the most pertinent information. Conciseness prevents the resume from becoming an interviewing crutch. If your resume is so long that it tells practically everything about you, there will be little of importance left for you to say during an interview. A concise resume prompts questions and leaves room for elaboration.

HOW TO USE A RESUME

Most people don't know how to use a resume. Ideally, individuals with mediocre qualifications and unsophisticated interviewing abilities would do well to discard the resume as soon as it is completed to avoid relying upon it as a crutch when interviewing. It will have served its most important purpose, and that is to help them to get mentally organized for the interview.

Be discriminating in distributing your resume. It should be handed out only upon request and, even then, reluctantly. What a prospective employer does not know about you will cause him to ask questions, giving you an opportunity to elaborate upon your background and qualifications and thus resulting in a more stimulating interview. Resumes can prompt questions, but they cannot give complete answers or put the emphasis where it should be in the context of an interviewer's concern or interest at a given moment in time. Thus, inaccurate conclusions can be drawn from the resume, leading a prospective employer to believe that you are overqualified or too versatile, and perhaps too high priced, for the job in question.

Don't hand out your resume at a job interview unless it is specifically and emphatically demanded of you, or unless, after the interview, you feel confident that it would provide a good summary of what was discussed. If you *do* give the interviewer a resume, let him read it thoroughly and completely without any interruption or distraction by you. Don't sit in your chair and watch him. Take the pressure off him by excusing yourself to go to the rest room or by walking away from your chair and gazing out the window.

If the interview turns out to be an extremely successful one, with seemingly good prospects that you can get the job, and the interviewer asks you for a resume, don't reveal to him that you have one readily available. Instead, say that you do not have a resume with you but that you will promptly prepare one for him and hand-deliver it or mail it to him. Then, go home and retype your current resume, adding or deleting whatever you think appropriate in light of the information you gained from the interview, and get it into his hands without delay. (A personalized resume, particularly a typed one, has a far more favorable effect than one which is printed with the obvious intent of mass distribution.) After you are reasonably certain that the interviewer has had time to receive and read your resume, follow up with a telephone call to see if any additional clarifying information is needed. If more information is desired, try to arrange another meeting.

The same basic considerations apply to the mailing of resumes as generally apply to their use in the interview. In short, be very selective as to when and to whom you mail your resume.

Sometimes, in an effort to be helpful, a friend or acquaintance will ask you to give him a handful of resumes so that he can pass them out to others on your behalf. Don't do it! Instead, ask him to give you the names of the people he has in mind, ostensibly to save him the trouble of mailing, but actually to allow you to establish contact with them by your own methods. Be firm about this and don't yield. If you don't know who has your resume, you lose a degree of control over your job campaign and thereby may miss a good opportunity.

The only way a resume should be used in a direct mail campaign is to accompany a letter of availability, prepared in the form and manner suggested in Chapter 9. The letter of availability is sent to distantly located companies which cannot be visited without considerable expense and effort, as discussed in Chapter 4.

If a prospective employer tells you on the telephone that he will not see you until you send him a resume, tell him that you will prepare one right away, especially for him. Be sure to imply that you do not have a ready-prepared resume. Try to arrange a meeting with him at his earliest convenience, setting the exact date and time while you have him on the phone and while he is fully aware that you are anxious to make a special effort to meet with him.

Don't ever attach a resume to an employment application form as a substitute for filling out the form. This never fails to offend a prospective employer.

*   *   *

Job hunting and organizing for it, including preparation of the resume, is not easy. What is at stake in exchange for your hard work is a job — your career — which is the basis of your self-respect and your livelihood and which represents at least one third of your life during your working years. Results! That's all that counts! And a well prepared resume helps you to build a case as to why someone should hire you and pay you a good salary.

"We should be careful to get out of an experience only the wisdom that is in it — and stop there; lest we be like the cat that sits down on a hot stove-lid. She will never sit down on a hot stove-lid again—and that is well; but also she will never sit down on a cold one any more."

—Mark Twain

6
Interviewing:
Strategy for Winning

For some, the most dreaded phase of job hunting is the interview. You are at center stage before an emotionless and critical audience. You are on trial before a tough-minded judge, and there is no jury. You are totally on your own, with no one to lean on. And the stakes are high; because unless you get good marks on the interview, there will be no job offer. But there is no need to despair over this, for most people, including employers, don't know how to handle an interview, and this makes them uncomfortable in an interviewing situation. You, however, will have a substantial advantage over most interviewers and other job seekers, because you are going to learn everything you need to know about how to conduct yourself in two types of interviews — the advice interview and the job interview.

While the advice interview usually is conducted on an

easygoing, low-key level, the job interview often becomes a stress test. Some interviewers like to see how you react under the pressure of hard-nosed interrogation. It isn't an adversarial situation; it *is* a test. Employers are neither devils nor demigods, but they must go to whatever extremes they feel are necessary and appropriate to find the right people when filling jobs. Just keep in mind that, when you enter the job market, you travel a two-way street; because the employer needs you as much as you need him.

Before continuing, let's consider your personal appearance for the interview. You don't have to be told that you should be clean and carefully groomed, but for the benefit of those who might need reminding, special attention should be given to the following:

- Hair should be neatly trimmed and in place.
- Shoes should be polished.
- Dress should be conservative and as well tailored as you can afford. For a man, a suit in navy blue or charcoal gray would be appropriate, either in solid color or with a not-too-bold pinstripe. If you are a woman, a dress, or preferably a suit, of classic (not trendy) design would do nicely. In either case, avoid plaids if at all possible. (Be sure that your clothes are not permeated with the lingering smell of tobacco smoke. And don't smoke during the interview, even if the interviewer does.)
- Fingernails should be neatly manicured (hands draw a lot of attention).
- Maintain good posture, both standing and seated.

These are the most prominent considerations regarding your appearance. Other less obvious ones will come to your attention and should be cared for. Every detail of your appearance, no matter how slight, is important.

As mentioned earlier, there are two kinds of interviews that will concern you: the advice interview and the job interview.

The advice interview was mentioned in Chapter 4, and we will examine it first.

THE ADVICE INTERVIEW

You will get advice interviews by writing letters (see Chapter 9) and making telephone calls to people you know, whether personally or not, and to whom you have been referred by others.

Although these interviews are arranged for the purpose of getting advice concerning your job-search program, you hope they will turn into job interviews. So be very personable when greeting the interviewer. Look him straight in the eye and smile; give him a firm handshake and say, "Hello, Mr. _____. I'm (first name) (last name). This is indeed a pleasure."

Start out by telling the interviewer why you are there, that you are in the process of looking for a job and are calling on certain people for advice. Be sure to emphasize, as you should have in your letter or on the telephone, that you do not intend to ask him for a job and that his advice is all that you are seeking. He may or may not come right out and ask what kind of advice he can give you. In any event, tell him that you would like to begin by taking a few minutes to tell him about yourself. Don't start with, "I was born in. . . ." He has neither the time for, nor the interest in, your complete autobiography. Begin, rather, by telling him briefly about your work experience and why you are in the job market. You might, and probably should, let him know something about your interests and activities when away from your work environment. Next, tell him what your objective is (chief financial officer, director of marketing, etc.) and briefly outline your strong points. Then guide him through your portfolio (see Chapter 4), slowly enough for him to take note of your accomplishments.

Having set the background, you now are ready to ask his advice about some specific matters, which is the reason you gave for requesting the interview. Let him know that, while you are concentrating on companies in the industry where most of your experience lies, you are seriously considering contacting companies outside of your industry. Ask his opinion as to whether your opportunities and chances of success would be greater in your own industry or in some other one. And ask if he thinks your opportunities would be even greater if you were to relocate to some other geographical area. There may be other questions you can think of; but the point is that you initially requested an interview because you were in need of advice, so be sure to ask for it with specific questions.

Before the interview comes to an end, show the interviewer the list of companies you have compiled and included in your portfolio. Ask him which of the companies he thinks you should contact and if he can think of any others that should be on your list. If he knows the right people at any of the companies, and gives you their names, ask if he would give you an introduction, either by letter or telephone. If he appears unwilling to do this, or even uncomfortable about it, ask for permission to mention his name. In any event, be sure to make it clear that you are not asking for his endorsement. If he refuses both an introduction and permission to use his name, ask rather lightly, "Then how can I manage to get through to him when his secretary answers the telephone?" This should cause him to reconsider and at least allow you to use his name when you write.

Now, here is an important point to remember when interviewing, whether it be for advice or for a job: never monopolize an interview by doing a monologue. Be sure to ask enough questions to keep the interviewer involved and to give him the feeling that he is in control of the interview.

You should arrange as many advice interviews as you possibly can. Try to have at least one or, even better, two each day. There is little doubt that some worthwhile suggestions will come out of them. But remember, advice is not what you actually are seeking. You at least want referrals to the right people in other companies. And most of all, you hope that at some point during the meeting the interviewer will begin to match your qualifications against a position which currently is available in his own company or which, while under consideration, is as yet non-existent. He might even consider creating a new position suggested by his perception of your particular strengths and qualifications. If this happens, the advice interview will evolve into a job interview, which we will discuss next so that you will be prepared to handle this transition.

THE JOB INTERVIEW

The job interview differs from the advice interview in that (1) it generally is conducted in a somewhat formal manner as compared to the rather casual atmosphere of the advice interview, and (2) the interviewer sets the pattern of the job interview and asks most of the questions. However, later in this chapter you will learn certain strategic techniques which will enable you to maintain control of the interview and to steer it in the direction you want it to follow. You will learn to do this with subtlety so that the interviewer will not be aware that you are in control. And in the next chapter we will cover most of the sensitive questions you will be asked during an interview and learn how to field them with specific answers. But before we get involved with strategy and questions, which are areas of concern in a normal, or standard, interview, let's consider what you would do in a situation where your interview time is unexpectedly cut short.

THE BRIEF JOB INTERVIEW

Any one of a number of circumstances could occur unexpectedly to cause the time alloted for an interview to be shortened. If this happens to you, make every effort to reschedule the meeting, both out of consideration to the interviewer and for your own best interest. If the interviewer will not postpone the meeting, ask him how much time you have and what subject in particular he would like you to address in the short time available. You will, of course, start out by talking about the specific area of interest he has indicated; but just as soon as you can, and as smoothly as possible, shift into a discussion of your strong points as described in your functional resume. Do not read from your resume. Don't even have it in front of you. But be familiar enough with it for your memory to be able to rely upon it as a guide while you highlight your strong points. However, *do* use your portfolio if there is any documentation in it of the examples you use to illustrate your strengths.

Below is an example of how your presentation of your strong points should proceed during a brief interview. The example is a bit lengthy, but necessarily so in order to give you the feel of how to handle yourself in such a situation. Don't be shy about blowing your own horn. No one else is going to do it for you, and the stakes here are high. Refer to the functional resume in Appendix A, and notice how the following narrative tracks the examples given in the resume:

"With fourteen years of good, solid experience behind me, I have developed a lot of skills, but basically I'm a top-level planner with strong managerial and leadership qualities. I also am creative and have demonstrated excellent foresight capabilities. I have a great deal of initiative and am tactfully persuasive. Since our time is somewhat limited, it probably would be a good idea for me to give you just one example of my effectiveness in each of these areas. Suppose I start with an example of what I have done as a top-level planner.

"Ever since I was made Controller of Midwest Steel Company in 19___ , I have been involved in top-level planning, and I have become very adept at it since I became Vice President of Finance and Accounting for the company three years ago. As an example, I recommended to the board of directors a new dividend policy which was designed to increase the market value of the common stock to a level in excess of its book value. The dividend was increased as I recommended and the market value of the common stock improved as expected, obviously as the result of my planning. [Now take your portfolio in hand.] Here is a copy of the memorandum I prepared for the Chairman of the Board. I don't expect you to read it, but it does document my point.

"I indicated earlier that creativity is one of my strongest capabilities. Late in 19___, through successful negotiating, Midwest Steel obtained a contract-termination settlement from another company which amounted to $225,000,000. As Financial Vice President, I devised a rather unique method of accounting for this transaction and developed a strategy for income tax purposes which minimized the tax consequences to the company. These were recognized as innovations, since this particular type of transaction was unprecedented in the steel industry. This is an example of my creative ability. [Again turn to your portfolio.] Here is a clipping of an article from *The Wall Street Journal* reporting my comments to the New York Society of Security Analysts concerning the transaction and the tax accounting applied to it.

"Now let's talk about foresight and initiative. I have realized for a long time that in order to improve, or even to maintain, the credit ratings of Midwest Steel Company's senior securities and to increase the attractiveness of its common stock to investors, more attention would have to be devoted to investor relations activities. As Financial Vice President, and with these objectives in mind, I recommended and implemented an intensive investor relations program to increase the demand for new issues of our common stock, which now sells at a premium. As a result, the credit ratings of the senior securities of the company were upgraded, meaning that it now can borrow funds at lower interest rates. So you see, I had the foresight to recognize the problem in time and the initiative to do something about it. This is just one example of my capabilities in these areas. Let me show you these letters from Moody's and Standard & Poor advising the company of the upgrading of their ratings of its bonds and preferred stocks. The main reason given was the effect of the new investor relations program.

"Lastly, I would like to talk about my persuasive talents. Several years ago, shortly after I had been promoted to the position of Vice President of Finance and Accounting at Midwest Steel, we set out to obtain the required consent of the shareholders to amend the Articles of Incorporation concerning a matter having severe financial implications to the company. We obtained the "swing" votes necessary to achieve this critical amendment due solely to my personal attention to one of our largest and most influential shareholders, whose initial attitude toward our objective was decidedly negative. This was, indeed, an accomplishment of which I am very proud and is an example of my persuasiveness.

"Well, that's a brief overview. As I have said, the most outstanding of my many strong points are top-level planning, creativity, foresight, initiative and persuasiveness, and I have fourteen years of broad and in-depth involvement in financial management. How do you think these demonstrated capabilities would fit your needs?"

No matter what his answer is to this question, quickly try to arrange for another interview:

"I realize how busy you are, and, believe me, I appreciate the time we've had to talk today, even though it was short. Could we schedule another meeting for next week so that we can go into this in more depth and consider ways that I might be able to help you here?"

When you call attention to the brevity of your interview, the interviewer, in all likelihood, will feel some guilt for having rushed you and probably will agree to arrange another meeting, unless this first interview was a complete disaster. Sometimes that can happen before you become more experienced in interviewing. If it does, put it behind you and go to other interviews. Your interviewing techniques and your self-confidence will improve as you move ahead.

INTERVIEWING STRATEGY

Interviewing is not a single, one-shot thrust at a target to be followed by retreat. It is more like a battle in a major campaign, to be fought relentlessly until you win. You learn something from each encounter; and you do better at each interview than you did at the last one, until you find yourself moving smoothly and fluidly through your interviews with no surprises to catch you off guard.

As in any endeavor, there are certain rules of thumb you must keep in mind if your interviewing strategy is to be effective.

When interviewing, the ability to memorize is essential, not only with regard to the points you want to emphasize during the interview but to the exchange that takes place between you and the interviewer. This becomes increasingly important as the interview advances from one stage to another. That's why a call-back interview requires somewhat more preparation than the first one.

Your attitude toward the interviewer, and your overall perspective, will show through and can have a dramatic effect on the outcome of the interview. You must make the prospective employer aware of your interest in knowing what you can do to help him and how easy you are to get along with.

From time to time during the interview, interrupt yourself and ask the employer if you are addressing the areas in which he is interested. You want to be sure that you stay on the right track — *his* track — and that you don't get off on a spur line.

Also, watch his facial expressions and mannerisms. If he

frowns, raises an eyebrow or begins to tap his fingers on his desk, it's a sure sign that you have said something to disturb or puzzle him. These are question marks, and question marks are negatives. Therefore, get them out into the open right away by asking if you have said something that troubles him.

When you feel reasonably sure that the employer knows everything about you that he needs to know, and should know, in order to be able to evaluate you properly, then stop talking. Sometimes an interviewer will just sit and look at you in dead silence when you finish speaking. Don't let this tactic intimidate you into saying more than you intend to. Join him in his silence and look back at him as though you are waiting for him to say something. Don't babble.

Don't prejudge anything about the interviewer, the company or the job; and don't ever terminate an interview yourself. Keep it going until the interviewer brings it to a close or until an actual job offer is made.

If, when all is said and done, a job offer is not made and the employer adopts a "Don't call me, I'll call you" attitude, despite your efforts to arrange a follow-up meeting, then ask him directly if he thinks you are qualified for the job. He may be the kind of person who always avoids a confrontation, and, that being possible, you will want to get the issue out on the table immediately so that you will know where you stand with him. If it becomes unmistakably evident that you are not going to get a job offer, turn the job interview into an advice interview and ask for referrals to others who might counsel you on your job-search campaign.

Remember. You are selling in an interview, so be sure to talk about what you can do for the employer, not what he can do for you. Selling requires a special sense of the attitudes and reactions of the prospect. You should, therefore, as quickly as possible, formulate an understanding of the personality-type of the individual interviewing you. Get a feel for what the employer wants to hear from you and handle the interview accordingly. As soon as you are able, make a determination of his acceptance of you; and be aware that there are three specific levels of acceptance:

1. He may have a high degree of confidence in you.
2. He may need reassurance, in which case you should stress your past accomplishments and results.
3. He may be in complete doubt about you. In fact, he probably is—at least in the earlier stages of the interview. Therefore, put everything you have into the interview and don't be unduly modest about yourself.

Be sure to exhibit conviction and enthusiasm and show that you have a sense of humor. Be pleasant and relaxed. Knowledge helps you to do these things. You are, without doubt, quite comfortable with your knowledge of your field of specialization. You should, in addition, be familiar with the employer's company and its products or services. You can learn about the company, and what it does, by talking to people who work there and by doing some research at the library.

Be careful in your conversations with strangers on or about the employer's premises. Some employers (not many, I'm happy to say) are devious enough to "plant" someone to strike up a conversation with you just to find out what you *really* think about the company, the job, your ability to do it and the people who have interviewed you. If this should happen to you, be terse — and be positive.

Previous mention has been made of the importance of your getting and maintaining control of the job interview, and the techniques for accomplishing this are found throughout this chapter. There are at least three reasons for you to take this initiative:

First, employers usually are not trained for interviewing

and therefore are not very skilled at it, which is why they tend to be nervous and uncomfortable in that setting. They talk a lot, often using up as much as half the time allotted for the interview; so, in order to be sure that the employer gets the information and the impression of you that he should have to evaluate you properly, you must get control of the interview very early, and keep control, lest you be deprived of the opportunity to get your story across adequately.

Second, employers are busy people and will try to get through an interview as quickly as possible. Therefore, to avoid being shortchanged, you will have to manipulate the interview to make sure you get all the important points across in the time available.

Third, and last, the employer probably will find it difficult to make a decision as to whether to hire you and will resist doing so. Therefore, you must make it easy for him to make that decision by presenting yourself effectively. Be sure he understands that you are capable of doing the job, and project yourself as being compatible and easy to work with. He wants to fill the job, so be persistent with him and carefully nudge him into making up his mind.

This is where "building value" comes into play. In fact, it's the name of the game in maneuvering the employer off dead center. But what is it? Just what is meant by "building value"? Well, in this sense, it is a step-by-step process of bringing the employer to the realization that you are the man or woman for the job. You are able to do this through your knowledge of yourself and his company.

Knowing your own value enables you to deal from strength and gives you the self-confidence to avoid unnecessary compromise. Knowledge about the company will put you above other candidates. So do some extra work to prepare for your interview. Research the company, not superficially but in depth. Become fluent in reciting results-oriented examples of your previous accomplishments. Your familiarity with the company and its operations, as provided by your research, will enable you to relate these examples with a bias toward the company so that the employer will recognize your potential value to it and to himself.

*   *   *

Interviewing can be fun or it can be devastating. It can be an exhilarating challenge or a depressing nemesis. But remember, one-third of your life during your working years is spent at your job. Your work, then, must be satisfying to you or both your mental and physical health will suffer. So if you feel that interviewing and the hours spent preparing for it are drudgery, or if you think you can take shortcuts, just remember what is at stake: your health, your time (lots of it) and your income.

It is entirely possible to do well at your job even if you are unhappy in it, but you will resent the time you put into it; and your health may be adversely affected, as well as your income. Clearly, then, it isn't enough just to be good at your work. Human relations is the most important facet in getting along in a job, so you must be enthusiastic and cooperative at all times. But you can't be that way if you are unhappy because you are in the wrong job. Therefore, be diligent and sincere in your preparation for interviewing so that you will be at your best; because only if you know what you have to offer, and are able to sell it, will you have any assurance of getting the job that is right for you.

"The most immutable barrier in nature is between one man's thoughts and another's."

—William James

7

Sensitive Interview Questions

During a job interview, the interviewer, by one means or another, must evaluate your personality and demeanor and obtain information about your background, your attitudes, your personal history and your overall qualifications for the job. The most commonly used techniques are: requiring the completion of a job application form prior to the interview; creating pressure or stress situations; and generally encouraging you to reveal more than is necessary, or advisable, about yourself. You should be prepared and able to recognize these techniques and learn to be artful in turning them around to your own benefit.

If you know in advance, or can find out, who will be interviewing you, it would be worthwhile to learn as much as you can about him or her prior to the interview.

Regardless of the specific techniques used by the interviewer, he will implement them by soliciting your answers to carefully planned questions. You should give some forethought to this. Below is a list of typical questions you can expect during a job interview and, following each, a brief indication of what the interviewer *really* wants to know. Be sure you are able to cope with the types of situations created by these questions. There are no pat answers. Although suggested responses are given for some of the trickier questions, you must work out your own answers to fit your particular circumstances. And be aware that the longer your answer to a question, the more it reflects your sensitivity to it.

1. **"Why do you want to work here?"**
   Wants to know: How much you know about the company.

2. **"Why do you want to switch to this field?"**
   (Assuming that the job is in a field that would be new to you.)
   Wants to know: Whether you have a sincere interest in, or any inapparent qualifications for, a job in a field which is unfamiliar to you.
   Suggested answer: "When comparing jobs in one field with those in another, it often is found that the functional aspects of certain jobs are much the same even though the fields are different. I would like to hear more about the job we have been discussing today, because that may be the case here. If that is so, then I would like very much to consider making such a change."

3. **"What caused you to leave your last job?" or "Why do you want to change jobs?"**
   Wants to know: Whether you were fired and, if so, why. Also, whether or not you get along well with your associates.
   Suggested answer: "I wanted [or want] a position offering greater challenges and opportunities."

4. **"How long have you been out of work?"** (Assuming you currently are unemployed.)
    Wants to know: Whether you are a stale commodity in the job market, indicating that no one else has had an interest in hiring you.
    Suggested answer: "Actually, I don't think of myself as being out of work, because looking for a job keeps me busy on a full-time basis." (The objective here is to avoid a quantification of the length of time you have been unemployed, if at all possible.)

5. **"What have you been doing since you have been unemployed?"** (Assuming you are unable to avoid giving a specific answer to question 4.)
    Wants to know: Whether you are an idler; how you react to set-backs.
    Suggested answer: "As I have said, I took the time to organize a very detailed job-search campaign, and carrying it out has kept me quite busy."

6. **"How do (did) you like working at _____ company?" "Why?"**
    Wants to know: Whether you are a malcontent. (Answer this question in very positive terms.)

7. **"Would you rather have (have had) another job, a different one, in that company?"**
    Wants to know: Whether you have the initiative to try to make a change.
    (If you are claiming that a desire for increased responsibilities or a better chance for advancement is your reason for seeking a change in employment, your answer to this question should be in the affirmative.)
    Suggested answer: "Yes, and I have asked several times to be transferred to another department where I could make fuller use of my capabilities

and where chances for advancement would be more favorable. However, more than six months have past since my last request and nothing has materialized."

8. **"What do (did) you dislike the most about your present (last) job?"**
    Wants to know: Whether you are a complainer or a malcontent. (Be careful with this one.)
    Suggested answer: "It isn't (wasn't) challenging enough."

9. **"Have you ever made any suggestions to your management?" "What were they?" or "Have you ever wanted to make any suggestions to your management but didn't?" "What were they and why not?"**
    Wants to know: Whether you have initiative, aggressiveness and enthusiasm. (This is not a frequently asked question, but be prepared in case it comes up. Don't admit that you have never made a suggestion to management. If necessary, make up something, but have it ready beforehand.)

10. **"Tell me about the best boss you have ever had." "The worst."**
    Wants to know: Whether you are a complainer or a "soft-toucher".

11. **"Tell me about the most difficult task you have ever had to do."**
    Wants to know: Your assessment of what constitutes a difficult assignment as related to job challenges.

12. **"If you could have any job you want, what would it be?"**
    Wants to know: Whether you are dissatisfied with your established career.

13. **"If you were selecting someone to fill this job, what kind of person would you choose?"**
    Wants to know: How self-confident and aggressive you are.
    Suggested answer: "Someone well qualified — just like me."

14. **"What do you do in your spare time?"**
    Wants to know: Whether you are a loafer; because, if you are, you probably will loaf on the job.

15. **"How is your health?"**
    Wants to know: Whether you are in poor health or are a hypochondriac. If either is the case, it may reflect in your performance and cause excessive absence.
    Suggested answer: "My health is excellent."

    (There should be no other answer to this question. Employers are accustomed to this response. Saying that your health is merely good will signal that there may be a problem. So if you think you can manage to make it to work every day, say that your health is excellent.)

16. **"If you could live your last ten or fifteen years over again, what changes would you make?"**
    Wants to know: Whether you lack direction.
    Suggested answer: "None!" (Be positive.)

17. **"Tell me about the greatest disappointment you have ever had."**
    Wants to know: Whether you have had any failures. (Be careful with this one.)
    Suggested answer: "I guess I've been very fortunate, because I can't recall any major disappointments in my life. Except as a child, of course,

when little things take on such importance."

18. **"In your opinion, what could management do to help you function better as an employee?"**

    Wants to know: Whether you are a complainer or a malcontent.

    Suggested answer: "I believe that most employees could do a better job if management, in general, would communicate more with them." (Be sure to couch your answer in positive terms.)

19. **"How does your wife feel about your work?" "How would she feel about the job we are discussing here?"**

    Wants to know: Whether your wife is resentful of the demands of your job or if she is supportive of you.

20. **"Assuming I were to hire you for this job, how would you view your future here?"**

    Wants to know: How ambitious you are and/or whether you might be a threat to him or to the status quo of the organization.

    Suggested answer: "As I see it, my future would depend upon yours. So the more I could do to help you, the better it would be for me."

21. **"What are some of your pet peeves?"**

    Wants to know: Whether pettiness is characteristic of you. (Be careful how you answer this. Light humor is safest.)

    Suggested answer: "Well, the first thing that comes to mind is never being able to find my tools after my son has used them."

22. **"Are you considering any other positions at the present time?" "How do they compare**

with this one?"

Wants to know: The strength of his bargaining power.

23. **"What, to you, is the meaning of success?" "By what standards do you judge it?"**

Wants to know: Your sense of values. (Answer by stating "hard" values, not "soft" ones. Hard values are *money, power, prestige,* etc. Soft values are *job satisfaction, happiness, having friends,* etc.)

24. **"Almost everybody likes to criticize. What is there about you that people find to criticize?"**

Wants to know: Your faults. Also, your answer may indicate how sensitive or thin-skinned you are.

Suggested answer: "Nothing of any significance."

25. **"What characteristics do you generally criticize in other people?"**

Wants to know: How well you get along with others. (Be careful in answering this one.)

Suggested answer: "Nothing much. After all, just because someone is different from me doesn't necessarily mean that he's wrong and I'm right."

26. **"What factors have kept you from progressing as rapidly as you feel you should have?"**

Wants to know: Whether you make excuses for yourself.

Suggested answer: "None that I am aware of, because I think I have progressed very well."

27. **"Have you ever fired anyone?" "How did you feel about it?"**

Wants to know: How tough you can be.

Suggested answer: "Yes, I have had to fire people.

[If you are at the supervisory or management level, this should always be your answer to this question.] I don't think anybody enjoys firing someone. I try, first, to find another spot for the employee where I think he can be effective. Otherwise, I do what has to be done for the benefit of the organization and let it go at that."

If you have never been in a supervisory position, your answer should be something like this: "I've never had anyone reporting directly to me, so I have never been in a position to hire or fire people. However, I have been asked my opinion on such matters and I have given it objectively."

28. **"What else do you think I should know about you?"**
    Wants to know: Anything else about you that has not been revealed by other questions. (Be careful. This is a potential trap, so don't talk too much. Use this as an opportunity to bring out any positive information about yourself that you haven't been able to cover in response to other questions.)

Here are several other typical, yet more difficult, questions. Although they are direct and straightforward, with no hidden meanings, the answers should be thought out very carefully.

29. **"Tell me about yourself."**
    In order to save time, ask what specific areas the interviewer would like you to address — personal, academic or career background — and be prepared with a thumb-nail sketch about yourself in each of these areas.

30. **"Wouldn't this be a career change for you?"**
    Emphasize that, even though the job is somewhat different from any you have had before, your

capabilities and talents are readily transferrable to its requirements.

31. "What are some of your weaknesses?"
Answer by saying that you are not aware of any weaknesses and that no one has ever mentioned any significant ones to you. Pass it off lightly if you can. For instance, if you happen to be a bit overweight, you might say, "My weakness is obvious, I think. I enjoy good food."

32. "What are your strong points?"
For a suggested answer to this question, refer to the section entitled "The Brief Job Interview" in the previous chapter. In the example given there, we cited good managerial and leadership qualities, creativity, foresight, initiative and persuasiveness as being among your greatest strengths. Use the same basic narrative suggested in that section, modified as appropriate, to answer this question, making the most of the opportunity to expand upon your strong points with specific examples.

33. "Tell me about your failures."
Answer by saying, "There have been none that I can recall. I have always been successful at anything I have ever attempted."

34. "You don't seem to have the technical knowledge for this job. How would you be able to handle it?"
Point out that you have the basic business and management skills, which are readily transferable to any situation, and that you can quickly acquire whatever technical knowledge you may lack.

35. "Isn't this job below your ability level?"
This can be answered by saying, "That may be

true, but if this is the only position currently available in your company, I would consider it very seriously as an opportunity to establish a foothold with an eye to future possibilities."

36. "How much money do you want?"
If this comes up early in the interview, try to avoid the discussion by saying that you would have to know more about the job and its responsibilities before you could evaluate it in terms of compensation. (Dealing with this question when it occurs late in the interview, or in connection with an actual job offer, will be covered in the next chapter.)

37. "We were thinking in terms of a younger person for this job."
Legally, this concern is not allowed to be voiced. Nevertheless, it does enter into hiring decisions and there is no way to prevent that. Sometimes it comes right out into the open, but more often it is introduced with artful obliqueness. In any event, be positive in your response and, with a smile, say something like this: "I know we're not supposed to talk about that, but I'm glad you brought it up. Actually, I have more than ___ years to give to a company, and I can be a balancing factor in a young organization. As an added bonus, my experience and on-the-job education has been paid for by someone else, so that would be a bargain to your company at any price."

38. "We have all we need to evaluate you for this position. We'll be in touch with you."
Show your continued interest and self-confidence by asking the interviewer if he could have someone show you a part of the plant or a new product before you leave. Ask if there is anyone else in the

organization you should talk to. Keep in control by suggesting that you will call him in a few days. And finally, ask if, from all that he has learned about you, he still is considering you as a candidate for the job. His answer will help you to plan your next move.

It is essential that everything you say and do at the interview presents you in the best possible image compatible with the truth. You must keep in mind that the interviewer is concerned with finding out whether:

- You have shown consistent interest in a particular vocational area or career objective.
- Your education, employment history and other developmental areas show continuous application of effort.
- Your employment history shows maturity, responsibility, achievement and progress.
- Your experience has included any of the activities involved in the job for which you are being considered, in the event you do not possess the specific background desired.
- You reveal mature and realistic attitudes toward yourself and others rather than resentments and vengefulness.

It should be reemphasized that there are no pat answers to the questions covered in this section and that appropriate responses must be developed and practiced with great care. The following guidelines will help you to create the best impression possible and to avoid the kinds of difficulties which could result from thoughtless answers:

- Listen carefully to the question. Be sure that you understand precisely what is being asked.
- Take time to sift through and organize all the facts available to answer the question.
- Then, answer the question. Be direct and to the

point, and be positive. Give only as many facts as needed to answer the question, being careful not to stumble into any sensitive or difficult areas. You must, of course, be truthful, but you do not have to volunteer information which could detract from the values you are attempting to build. Therefore, don't divulge any negative information unless it is absolutely unavoidable.

- Use every opportunity to emphasize and reemphasize your capabilities and major strengths, as well as any related accomplishments, indicating their potential value to the position being discussed.

Your answers to questions asked during the interview should be unfaltering and exude self-confidence. They don't have to be precise or exact, but they must be closely relevant to the core of the questions.

When the interview progresses to the point of, or even near to, a job offer, questions about compensation will arise. The next chapter, concerning salary negotiation, will take you through an entirely different series of questions and suggest how to handle them.

"Don't talk unless you can improve the silence."
                                              —Old Vermont proverb

8

Negotiating Salary with Confidence

It is surprising how passive most of us become when the question of compensation arises in a job interview. It would be safe to guess that 90 percent of all executives have never attempted to negotiate their own salaries. Even interviewers, for the most part, are not very skilled or astute when it comes to salary negotiation and are as uncomfortable with it as job candidates are.

It is important for you to realize that you will not lose a job opportunity by attempting to negotiate your salary. On the contrary, you are more likely to enhance the employer's esteem for you by demonstrating that you are a willing and able negotiator. Most employers are anxious for newly hired employees to be happy and satisfied with the conditions of their employment and will try to meet reasonable demands unless restricted by budgets, company policy or a potential morale problem. Therefore, you can and should enter into salary negotiation with confidence when the employer broaches the question of compensation.

Generally, when an interviewer raises a question concerning salary, he does not expect a direct answer, because the intent of the question usually is merely to initiate negotiation of the salary. Therefore, don't feel bound, in this case, to respond to direct questions with direct answers.

It is a point of fact that in more than 60 per cent of the times that employers ask the question, "How much?", job applicants will understate the amount of salary they really want. On the other hand, when employers are placed in the position of having to reveal what they are willing to pay for a job, they tend to overstate the amount. Therefore, it is *always* to your advantage to answer direct salary questions in such a way as to turn those questions back to the interviewer.

A basic principle in the art of salary negotiation is, if at all possible, to postpone or delay any discussion of salary until the following points have been well established:

- The responsibility requirements and reporting level of the position.
- Your value to the employer in terms of your ability to meet the responsibility requirements of the job.
- Your future prospects with the company.
- Your compatibility as a work associate.
- That the job is yours, subject only to arriving at an agreement on compensation.

Questions about salary may come up at any time. They may arise early, midway, or late in the interview. In the latter event, and by that time, your potential value to the employer probably has been well established. Depending upon when during the interview these questions may occur, there are slight variations in the way they should be handled, and, subtle though these differences may be, it is extremely important that you take note of them and understand them.

Before we continue, let me caution you never to raise the question of salary yourself. Don't ask how much the job pays unless you have received a definite job offer — not merely a suggestion of one — and the salary has not been mentioned. Doing so would give the impression that your primary concern is money. While this may be true, you don't want the employer to know it. You also may be getting into the salary question before he is ready to handle it.

If you do find it necessary to be the first to mention salary, and the employer's response is disappointing to you, act perturbed and say, "I was thinking of a higher figure than that." He will ask what you have in mind, after which you should proceed with negotiation of the salary, using the applicable techniques described later in this chapter.

Now, let's examine ways to handle the various salary questions as they may arise at different times during the interview.

EARLY SALARY QUESTIONS

In the early stages of the interview, neither you nor the employer knows enough about the other to make a relative determination of salary level. You have not yet established your value to the employer, nor do you know enough about the responsibilities of the job. Any discussion of salary at this stage of the interview might very well result in a loss of a job opportunity, because everything would hinge upon salary considerations alone. Therefore, it is important to politely deflect any attempts at salary discussion and defer them until late in the interview.

Any of the questions which appear below might arise in the early stages of the interview. Some of them are quite similar to one another, to the extent that they appear to be almost identical. But there are, in those instances, subtle differences, and the differences call for slight variations in the answers. Therefore, you will notice that certain of the suggested responses are somewhat repetitive of those given for other questions. This is unavoidable, however, if the suggested answers are to be sufficiently complete in order to be in full context with the corresponding questions.

As you study the following questions and suggested responses, try to adapt the responses to your own situation so that you will be comfortable with any of the questions that might arise.

1. **"How much are you making now?" (or "How much were you making in your last job?" if you are currently unemployed.)**

   Study the following suggested ways to sidestep this question. The one you choose will depend, of course, upon your level of comfort in using it and how well it fits the interview situation as it has developed.

   Approach (a) — Worth more than the job pays.
   Suggested response: "Mr. _____ , I would be glad to answer that question, but actually I'm worth a lot more than you would be willing to pay me and I can show you why. First, however, I want to be sure that I correctly understand the position you are thinking about. You are looking for someone with a comprehensive knowledge of financing methods. Is that correct?"

   [Pause here for a moment to let him respond.]

   "Some of my greatest accomplishments have been in acquisitions and sale and lease-back arrangements. I'd like to give you a few brief examples of the financing deals I have structured in those areas."

   [Pause again and wait for his expressed or tacit approval to continue. Never let the employer feel that he is not in control of the interview.]

   If you have done adequate research prior to the interview, you should be aware of the company's specific interests and thereby be able to tailor your examples to fit those interests. Otherwise, your discussion will have to be along more general lines. Now, to continue . . .

"All right, then, let me tell you about a problem I encountered in . . . ."

After answering any questions, ask the employer about his successes or problems in the areas you have addressed, and listen attentively. You now have the interview back on track and away from the question of salary.

Approach (b) — Establish responsibilities.
This approach is suitable if you are seeking a position with greater responsibilities in a reasonably similar line of work.

Suggested response: "I would be glad to give you that information, Mr. _____. However, I'm not sure it would be entirely fair to do so, and let me tell you why I say that. You see, one of the main reasons I am considering a change in jobs is that I believe I am ready for significantly greater responsibilities. So let's first identify the duties and responsibilities of this job, as you perceive them now, and then we will be better equipped to discuss what they are worth to you. Are you agreeable to that?"

[Wait for him to respond before you continue.]

"Now, as I understand the position you have in mind, you are looking for someone with considerable knowledge of various financing methods. Am I right? Well, some of my greatest accomplishments have been in acquisitions and sale and lease-back arrangements. I'd like to give you a few examples of some of the financing deals I have structured in those areas. Let me tell you about a problem I encountered in . . . ."

The above example assumes that the interviewer impresses you as being less than willing to talk about himself. It is always good, if possible, to bring the interviewer actively into an exchange of thoughts; so, if he seems at all willing to discuss his own problems and experiences, invite him to do so by modifying the above response in the following manner:

"Now, it is my understanding that you are looking for someone with considerable knowledge of various financing methods. Is that accurate? Well, according to your annual reports you are beginning to expand your operations by acquiring other companies. What are some of the problems that you have encountered in that area?"

This latter approach — that is, getting the employer to open up with discussion of his own problems — will help you to determine which examples of your own accomplishments would be most effective in convincing him of your potential value to him.

Approach (c) — Principle: *never to discuss salary in the absence of a job offer.*

Suggested response: "Mr. _____ , one of my principles is never to discuss salary unless it's in reference to a position that actually has been offered to me. You understand that, I'm sure."

Then, get the interview back on track by continuing as follows:

"Now, it is my understanding that you are looking for someone with comprehensive experience in financing methods. Am I right? Well, some of my greatest accomplishments have been in acquisitions and sale and lease-back arrangments. I'd like to give you a few examples of the financing deals I have structured. Let me tell you about a problem I encountered in...."

Approach (d) — Looking for a position that pays $ _____ .

If the interviewer is firm in wanting to know your current or last salary, and it is clear that he will not continue without this information, try to side-step the question by giving him a salary *range* that would be satisfactory to you rather than an exact figure. Since he is only looking for a way to start the salary negotiation, this should satisfy him.

Suggested response: "Mr. _____ , I'm looking for a position with a salary potential of $50,000 to $55,000 in the next three to four years. [These salary limits are for illustrative purposes only. Use whatever salary levels seem appropriate under actual circumstances.] Of course, I don't know where this position fits within your salary structure. What would be the starting range for this job?"

This assumes that you are looking for an offer at least in the low forties. Your $50,000 to $55,000 range probably — and hopefully — is above the attainable starting salary for the job, but since you have not insisted on any guarantees for the future, you have given the interviewer the impression that you are willing to work hard for a higher future salary and that you are flexible with regard to a starting salary. If he responds with a starting figure — and he probably will — it is likely to be somewhat higher than the middle of his range. If it is below the range you have in mind, act as though you are disappointed and try to shift the conversation away from salary considerations by encouraging the interviewer to talk about his own situation in the following manner:

"I see. Well, before we go any further along those lines, I would like to ask a question. I have a great deal of admiration for the way your company has grown in its field. You are, of course, very much involved in international operations. Could you describe some of your current financing problems in that area?"

Approach (e) — Estimate your job worth.

Again, if the interviewer insists upon knowing your present or last salary, and it is obvious that he will not continue the interview until his question is answered, an alternative to Approach (d) would be to estimate the total worth of your present or last salary by adding to your base gross salary the estimated value of all your fringe benefits.

A full range of benefits could add as much as 30 percent to your base salary. Assuming that you arrive at a total of $40,000, for example, reply with something like the following:

"I figure my present [or last] job to be worth about $40,000 per year. Please understand, however, that what I am seeking is an appropriate level of compensation for my real value to whatever company I work for. I'm capable of handling greater responsibilities than I have in my present position. That's one of the reasons I'm considering a change, and I intend to keep searching until I find the right job. Can you tell me [or, can you tell me more] about the job you have in mind here?"

Now you are in a position to show how your new responsibilities would be substantially greater than your present or previous ones (assuming that to be the case); and, if you eventually are offered a job by this employer, you are prepared to substantiate that, because of the increased responsibilities, your current or last salary is irrelevant to the value of the position under consideration.

Now, on with other salary-related questions that might arise early during the interview:

2. "How much do you think you are worth?"

Suggested response: (Be tactful, polite, and serious.)
"Well, Mr. _____ , I think I'm worth a lot. I hope
you don't think I'm impertinent, because I am very
serious. I think I'm worth a lot because I'm going to
perform at my maximum level; and I think I can
convince you that I have a lot to offer at that level."

Then get the interview back on track as follows:

"But first, I want you to know that I have a great deal
of admiration for the way your company has grown
in its field. You are, of course, very much involved in
international operations. Can you describe some of
your current financing problems in that area?"

3. "How much would you expect to be paid for this job?"

This question could be asked in several slightly
different ways, such as: "How much do you want to
be paid for this job?" "How much do you think you
should be paid?" "How much would we have to pay
you?"

Suggested response: (For this answer, also, be
tactful, polite, and serious.)

"To be perfectly frank, Mr. _____ , I would expect
to be paid as much as I could get. I hope you don't
think I'm impertinent, because I'm very serious. I
would expect to be paid as much as I could get
because I would perform at my maximum level; and
I think I can convince you that I have a lot to offer at
that level. But first, let me make certain that I
correctly understand the position. You are looking
for a strong manager with substantial experience in
financing methods. Am I right? Well, some of my
greatest accomplishments have been in acquisitions
and sale and lease-back arrangements. I'd like to give
you a few examples of the financing deals I have

structured in these areas. I'll begin with a problem I encountered in . . . ."

4. "What is the minimum salary you would take to start?"

Suggested response: (Pause and act slightly puzzled before you answer.) "I'm sorry, but I'm afraid I don't understand. You see, since I have never thought about a job in terms of minimum effort, I tend not to think in terms of minimum compensation. I always work toward achieving maximum results, and that certainly is what you would expect of me. Likewise, I would expect maximum compensation. But if you don't mind, before we get into a discussion of that, I would like to get a clearer idea of the problems and responsibilities that go along with the job. For example, which of your goals are the most dependent upon expertise in finance?"

5. "You have been unemployed for quite a long time now, haven't you? What is the minimum salary you would accept to start?"

Suggested response: "Well, I don't feel like an unemployed person because, actually, I have been very busy with my job-search campaign. Frankly, I don't intend to take just any job that comes along. I plan to weigh a number of alternatives against my long-term career objectives. I'm putting a lot of effort into this, and I intend to continue until I feel that I have found the best available opportunity. I think you would agree that this is the best direction for me to take. As for minimum salary — well, I just don't think in terms of minimums. Since I always work toward achievement of maximum results, I naturally would expect maximum compensation. But, if you don't mind, before we get into a discussion of that, I would like to get a clearer idea of the problems and responsibilities that go with the job. For example, it was announced recently that you have entered into a joint venture with a Korean electronics company. What has been your experience in predicting changes in the value of the dollar in that country?"

6. "Aren't you overqualified for this job?"

Although it may not sound like it, this question actually is a stab at salary negotiation. Take time to explore with the interviewer possibilities of increasing the responsibilities of the job to more nearly fit your qualifications. Essentially, attempt to create a new position in the light of your availability.

Suggested response: "Let me address that question by first making it clear that starting salary is not my paramount concern. What I really find exciting are your corporate goals. It's important to me to be able to work at something that I believe in. Since you bring up the question of overqualification, you apparently are concerned about the level of compensation for the job. If it's agreeable with you, I would rather hold off on any discussion of money until you get to know more about me. I'm sure you will find me to be flexible in that regard." Then, get the discussion back on track and away from money with a question, such as the following: "I have a question I would like to ask you, if I may. What kinds of financial problems are you currently involved with in your international operations?"

MID-INTERVIEW SALARY QUESTIONS

For the same reasons as those pertaining to early salary questions, it also is important to sidestep any attempts to discuss salary midway through the interview. You and the employer have not yet learned enough about each other to make a relative determination of salary level, and, more importantly, you still have not established your value to the employer.

Any salary-related questions arising at this stage of the interview would be the same as those just considered in "Early Salary Questions". They were:

1. "How much are you making now?" (or "How much were you making in your last job?" if you are currently unemployed.)
2. "How much do you think you are worth?"
3. "How much would you expect to be paid for this job?"
4. "What is the minimum salary you would take to start?"
5. "You have been unemployed for quite a long time now, haven't you? What is the minimum salary you would accept to start?"
6. "Aren't you overqualified for this job?"

If any of questions No. 1 through No. 5 above arise midway through the interview, respond by looking the interviewer straight in the eye and asking:
"Does this mean you are going to offer me a job?"
The abruptness and directness of your question probably will ruffle him if he did not intend to make a job offer at this time, allowing you the opportunity to get the interview back on track with a discussion of responsibilities of the job or a question concerning problems encountered by the employer.

If, on the other hand, he acknowledges that his question was leading to a job offer, thank him and proceed to enlarge upon the job responsibilities until you feel that you have a good understanding of them and that you are sure the employer is fully cognizant of your potential value to him. Then try to get him to make a salary offer by saying something like this:
"You mentioned money earlier, Mr. _____. Now, taking into consideration the duties and responsibili-

> ties we have covered, what do you think the job is
> worth?"

What you have done is to deflect a premature attempt at salary negotiation and held it off until later in the interview when your value has been established.

Now let us consider question No. 6, the last one on the list. It calls for a different approach than that suggested above. When the question of overqualification (which, in reality, is a money-related question) arises midway through the interview, don't treat it as though it were a job offer. Because it is only indirectly related to the salary issue, placing the question in the context of a job offer would leave the interviewer puzzled, to say the least. Therefore, your response to a question of overqualification, occurring midway through the interview, should be much the same as if it arose early in the interview. (See question No. 6 in "Early Salary Questions.")

LATE-INTERVIEW SALARY QUESTIONS

When you near the end of the interview, or after a series of interviews have taken place, and the employer attempts to hire you, salary negotiation becomes an issue of major importance. Your potential value to the employer has been factually established, and, therefore, you should enter into the negotiations with confidence and tactful aggressiveness. By no means should you take a passive position at this phase of the interview. And remember, you will not lose a job opportunity by engaging actively in the negotiation of salary.

The questions concerning salary that will arise at this stage of the interview are much the same as those that might have been asked earlier. However, the responses will be different, because at this point it is important for both parties to come to grips with the critical issue of compensation. This is the last and most important hurdle toward the successful culmination of your job-search campaign.

We now will reconsider the responses to the questions in the light of these different circumstances.

1. "How much are you making now?"

If you are currently employed, and the duties and responsibilities of the new position are not significantly different from those of your present one, respond candidly and tactfully as follows:

"Mr. _____, I'll answer that question if I must, but let me emphasize the fact that I wouldn't be here today if I were entirely satisfied with my present salary; and, above all, I don't want it to be the determining factor of the salary for this job. What figure do you have in mind for the position we've been discussing?"

If you are currently employed and there are decided differences between the responsibilities of your current position and those of the one being discussed, respond with: "Well, Mr. _____, it isn't easy for me to answer your question because, under the circumstances, my present salary doesn't seem to be entirely relevant. You see, the responsibilities of this job are so different from those of my present one that comparing them would be similar to comparing apples and oranges, just as it would be to try to compare reasonable salaries for the two jobs. So I guess I really have to rely upon you. What do you think this position is worth?"

Or, alternatively, you might respond with something like the following, if you sense that your present salary is higher than this position would pay:

"My present salary is quite substantial, but I don't want that to rule out my being considered for this opportunity. You see, I'm mainly interested in my future prospects with your company. With that in mind, what do you think the job should pay?"

2. **"How much were you making in your last job?"**
This question would be asked, of course, only if the applicant is currently unemployed.

Suggested response: "The job, as you describe it, sounds terrific! And I know I could really make something of it. Now, I'm sure you have a perfectly reasonable salary structure and, regardless of what I made before, I think the most equitable thing to do would be to stick with your salary range. Assuming that you agree with that, what salary do you have in mind?"

3. **"How much do you think you are worth?"**

Suggested response: (Be tactful, polite, and serious.) "Well, Mr. _____ , I think I'm worth a lot. I hope you don't think I'm impertinent, because I really am very serious. I think I'm worth a lot because, as I believe I have shown you, I have a great deal to offer. What do you think would be a reasonable salary range for the responsibilities of this position?"

4. **"How much would you expect to be paid for this job?"**

Suggested response: "Well, Mr. _____ , I would expect to be paid as much as I can get based on my worth; and, frankly, I'm worth quite a lot. I hope you don't think I'm being impertinent, because I'm really very serious. I would expect to be paid as much as I could get because I would perform at my maximum level, and, as I believe I have shown you, I have a lot to offer at that level. What do you think I would be worth to you in this position?"

Or,

"I think it would be rather presumptuous of me to even suggest to you what the salary should be for this position. Can you tell me what the range is for the job?"

5. "How much do you need to live on?"
Suggested response: "Regardless of what my actual
needs are, Mr. _____ , I feel that I should be paid a
salary in line with what others with similar responsibilities are being paid. Tell me, what is the
approximate salary range for this job?"

**6. "What is the minimum salary you will take to
start?"**
Note that this question differs little from the previous
one, except that it is worded in such a way as to
allow you to maneuver the employer into the
position of having to address the maximum salary
level for the job.

Suggested response: (Assume a slightly perplexed
expression and take your time in answering.) "It
isn't easy for me to answer that question, Mr.
_____ , because I've never thought about a job and
compensation in those terms. You see, as I believe I
have shown you, I have always performed at my
maximum level in any job I have undertaken, and
that attitude, by all means, would extend to this job.
With that in mind, I would like to hear your thoughts
as to what the maximum pay level is for this job."

**7. "You have been unemployed for quite a long
time now, haven't you? If I were to offer you
this job, what is the minimum starting salary
you would accept?"**
This, of course, would be asked in this manner only if
you were without a job at the time.

Suggested response: "Well, I don't think of myself as
being unemployed because, actually, I've been
working very hard. You see, I don't intend to take
just any job that comes along but, rather, to weigh a
number of alternatives against my long-term career
goals. I'm expending a lot of effort in this direction,

and I'll keep at it until I feel sure that, of the opportunities available at the time, I have chosen the one that is best for me.

"As far as minimum is concerned, I've never thought about jobs and compensation in those terms. I believe I have shown you that I always perform at my maximum level in everything I undertake, and that attitude certainly would extend to this job. Tell me, Mr. _____ , what do you consider to be the maximum pay level for this job?"

By indicating your determination to wait to compare and select from several job opportunities, you give the impression that you are not so desperate for money that you have to take the first job that becomes available.

8. "Aren't you overqualified for this job?"

If the employer believes you are overqualified, he probably thinks you are expecting a higher salary than he is able to pay you. Try to get him to expand the responsibilities of the job to more nearly fit your qualifications. Then, come right to the point of his apparent real concern — money.

Suggested response: "Well, that may be true. I may be somewhat overqualified, but I don't think that has to be a deterrent to this discussion. You see, Mr. _____ , in most organizations there are likely to be certain staff people who are trying to handle more than their share of the responsibilities — people who are really overloaded with work. There may be someone like that in your organization whose duties are to some extent related to this job. If so, it might make good sense to redistribute certain duties and responsibilities, at the same time enhancing the importance of this position to the company.

"The fact is, Mr. _____ , that I presently am making

a substantial salary, but I don't want that to rule out my chances for this job. You see, my future prospects in your company are far more important to me than starting salary considerations. Actually, I'm very excited about your corporate goals. [Or whatever other facet of the business you deem appropriate to highlight here.] It's important to me to be able to really believe in the objectives of an organization I work for. Now, with all this in mind, what are your thoughts as to my value to you in this job? I think you will find me to be quite flexible."

9. **"We couldn't pay you anywhere near as much as someone else could."**
This would be a situation in which the employer thinks you are very much overqualified for the job, *and actually you are*, but you are excited about the future prospects of the position. Your response, in this case, should be as follows:

"Mr. _____, I would like to ask you a question that is very relevant to that statement. You have learned quite a lot about me by now. Based on my background and qualifications, what salary do you think I could reasonably expect in today's market?"

In all likelihood, he will be honest and quote a figure which represents your true worth. If his figure sounds about right to you, proceed with:

"I think I agree with you. That's about what I think I'm worth right now, but, to be honest, I really don't believe I should expect to start at quite that high a salary."

This is an invitation to him to ask you what you think your starting salary should be, so pause to give him an opportunity to do so. Then, your response should be something like this:

"I'm not sure what my starting salary should be, Mr.

_____ . I like working at a job to which I can feel dedicated and that offers good prospects for the future. So you see, I don't think money is the most important consideration about a job. Therefore, I don't believe in taking a firm stand on the question of salary, and, for the right opportunity, I can be reasonably flexible. I believe, from what I have heard here, that the position we've been talking about is a great opportunity with good potential. I would like to have the job, and, for my part, I think we can arrive at a speedy and mutual agreement on the salary."

The only response the employer can make to this would be something like the following:

"Well, if you can be flexible, so can we. We should be able to work something out. Let's give it a try."

Thus far in our consideration of salary negotiation, your responses to questions and comments about compensation have been carefully worded in an attempt to force the employer to be the first to mention an actual salary figure. The reason for this strategy, you will recall, is that the employer tends to quote from the high end of the salary range, while the applicant generally quotes from the low end of the range. However, despite your best performance, the employer could outmaneuver you by whacking the ball into your own court with one or more of the following statements or questions:

10. **"This is a new position, so we're not sure where it should fit within our salary structure. What do you have in mind?"** (After you have tried to get the employer to commit himself on a salary figure.)

   Suggested response: "First, let me see if I can restate the responsibilities of the job. As I see it, I'll report to the Vice President of Finance. There will be a staff of six people reporting to me, including three very capable MBA's, and I will have overall responsibility for preparation of the corporate budget, keeping it current, monitoring expenditures, and preparation of the long-term forecast. Is that about right? Well, then, I feel confident that the salary structure throughout the entire company is quite equitable, so perhaps you can relate this job to another position in the company with comparable responsibilities. From that point of view, what do you think the salary should be for this new position?"

11. **"You must have some idea of how much you want."**

Suggested response: "Yes, I do. I want to be paid a salary that is in line with my value to you and the company as you see it. Now that I know you, and given the reputation of your company, I would feel perfectly comfortable in having you establish the salary on that basis, because I know you would be fair. You have a considerable amount of experience in the industry, and I have a great deal of respect for that. With all this in mind, then, what do you think the salary range would be for these same responsibilities in other companies of your size in this industry?"

Suppose, with all your efforts, you are unable to draw out a salary figure from the employer. The sparring back and forth cannot continue forever; and at some point you can expect the employer to come out, in both frustration and annoyance, with something like the following, which should get the negotiations moving toward a conclusion:

12. **"We've been kicking this around long enough! If you want this job, you've got to tell me how much we're going to have to pay you!"**
    At this stage, you had better give him some idea of a figure or, preferably, a range that you have in mind.

When you set a salary valuation level for a job,

always do it in terms of upper, middle, or low bracket, such as "in the mid-forties". However, try to set the salary level high enough to give the employer some flexibility to cut your figure back to a level which, in your estimation, would be acceptable to him but, hopefully, not less than about 90 percent of what you think the job is worth.

There are four good methods of asserting your evaluation of the worth of a job, depending upon your considered expectations of the employer's reaction and your own personal circumstances.

You may consider a job to be worth, say $30,000. The employer, however, may think of it in terms of a higher or lower value. You should allow for this likely difference in evaluation when you respond.

(a) The "probing" method

Suggested response: "Well, based on my understanding of the responsibilities, I would say the job should pay somewhere in the mid-forties. [Wait a moment for his reaction and, only if he acts disturbed, soften your statement.] . . . to perhaps the lower forties. Is that about what you think the job is worth?"

The employer may indicate agreement with you, in which case all that remains to be done is to pin the salary down to an exact amount (which, at this point, is an easy task) and close the interview by your acceptance of the position.

On the other hand, instead of agreeing with your assessment of the worth of the job, he may respond: "Oh, no! I'm sorry, but there is no way that we could pay that much." In which case you should counter with: "Well, then, how much *can* you pay?"

Since you have come forth with your assessment of what the job is worth, and the employer has expressed his disagreement, he now must give a direct answer as to what he will pay you, which probably will be higher than the amount he originally had in mind. Suppose his response is along the following lines:

"In this company, as in most companies of our size in the industry, the salary for this position should be in the mid-thirties up to, in extraordinary cases, perhaps the upper thirties."

Wait a thoughtful moment before you respond to this and, disregarding his mention of the lower end of the range, bounce back with:

"Mr. _____, I consider this job to be a great opportunity, and, to me, the starting salary is not the most important issue. The prospects for the future excite me the most. If I start out initially at only $39,000, and assuming maximum performance, what might the salary be in, say, two years from now?"

However he answers this question, you have reached a zone of mutual understanding. You now know approximately how much the employer is willing to pay you, he knows how much you would like to be paid, and you have a feel for future expectations. Everything is right for arriving at mutual agreement on the salary, and the chances are good that you will land near the top of the employer's range.

(b) The "range" method

Give the employer the salary range you have in mind, keeping the bottom of the range somewhat above the minimum salary you would consider to be acceptable. This should prompt him to counter with his own salary figure or range. If you are unhappy with what he comes up with, act surprised and tell him that you must have misunderstood the responsibilities and reporting level of the job. Tell him that the job apparently is not as important to the company as you understood it to be, and ask him to explain the responsibilities and reporting level once again. After he does that, assure him that you did, after all, correctly understand those aspects of the job. Let him know that you are flexible as far as salary is concerned and that you certainly want to be reasonable about it. Make it clear that it is not absolutely necessary for you to have the salary you originally asked for but that, if at all possible, you would like to get a little closer to it.

If he will not budge from his originally quoted figure, then tell him you would like to take time to think about what has been discussed. Arrange a definite time to get back to him with your decision and get his assurance that, when you do so, the job will be yours if you decide to accept it. Thank him for giving you so much of his time and politely take your leave. As soon as you can, prepare a thank-you letter. After allowing ample time for the letter to be delivered, call him and tell him that you are excited about the job, that you would like to start as soon as possible and that the salary is the only drawback. He may invite you back for further discussion, which would afford you an opportunity to narrow the difference in the salary figures. If he does not invite you back, reassure him of your flexibility as far as money is concerned and ask to meet with him again to try to work out something that would be acceptable to both of you. If he responds emphatically that he will not negotiate beyond his last offer, do not, by any means, say or do anything which might cause you to lose a job opportunity. Instead, ask if it would be agreeable for you to call in a month or two to talk about the situation as it may exist at that time.

If, however, you decide to take the job at the salary offered, make one final but tactful attempt to discuss the salary before accepting the position. If you clearly are unable to get a higher starting salary, try to negotiate a definite salary increase at the end of six months with a regular review at the end of one year.

(c) The "prospective" method

This is by far the safest way to broach the question of salary. It is a particularly good approach when you have decided that you want a job which has been offered to you but for which the starting salary is not up to your expectations.

The employer probably considers that salary increases for superior performance should be about 10-15 percent per year. A 10 percent increase per year for a period of three years would bring the salary up by about a third over the starting salary. A 15 percent raise each year over a three year period would amount to about a 50 percent increase over the beginning salary. With this in mind, mentally calculate the salary as it would be three years hence based upon your targeted starting figure. Then, respond by saying that, as the job has been described to you, and with superior performance, it appears that you might reasonably expect your earnings to reach the middle to upper fifties within a few years (assuming that $40,000 is your targeted starting salary) and that, if such is the case, you are more than willing to let the employer propose the starting salary. If he goes along with this, you can assume that the two of you are close in your assessment of the salary and that it will still be open for improvement in some manner in the future.

This approach tells the employer three things about you:

(1) That you intend to give superior performance.
(2) That you intend to work toward improving your performance over time.
(3) That you plan to be a long-term, dedicated employee.

Let's back up now. What if the employer does not agree with your projection of future earnings? In that case, he will tell you that you apparently are thinking of a higher starting salary than he can pay. If this comes about, ask:

"Well, then, what figure do you suggest for a starting salary?"

He probably will state an amount higher than that which he originally had in mind, but, if it is less than satisfactory to you, act puzzled and say:

"I was hoping that we could narrow the gap a

little more than that."

He may increase his offer, but if he doesn't, or if the increased offer still is not acceptable to you, then you should propose the possibility of expanding the responsibility requirements of the job. If he agrees with the proposal, you have a good chance of negotiating a higher starting salary. Therefore, carefully lead up to your recommended plan of action as follows:

"Mr. _____ , we both know that in most organizations there is likely to be at least one staff member who is trying to handle more than his share of the work — someone who is so overloaded that he is unable to give his best to any of the areas of his responsibility. You may have someone like that in your own organization whose duties and responsibilities are in some way related to this job. If that is the case, wouldn't it make good business sense to consider the possibility of redistributing some of the duties and responsibilities and, simultaneously, perhaps enhancing the importance of my position and allowing you to pay me a little more to start? An arrangement like that would be perfectly satisfactory to me. How do you feel about it?"

You may or may not be successful in getting the employer to take these steps to increase the responsibilities of the job and, likewise, the starting salary. Conditions such as you have described to him may not exist in his organization. Even if they do, he may not want to make the necessary changes, or there may be existing circumstances which would make it impossible or inadvisable for him to do so.

If your efforts to get the salary you want are

unsuccessful, tell the employer that you are sorry you could not get closer together on compensation and thank him for the interview. Go home and write him a thank-you letter. Then follow up with a telephone call in an attempt to arrange another meeting to discuss the salary. Impress upon him that you really want the job — that you are excited about it —but that you must first resolve the issue of the starting salary.

Carry whatever discussion that ensues from this to its logical end. There is a possibility that, at this point, the employer will increase his previous offer; but even if he does not, and you still want the job, try to negotiate a definite salary increase at the end of six months and a regular review at the end of one year before you accept the position.

(d) The "retroactive" method

This approach is effective when the starting salary has been advertised or otherwise made known to you.

If the employer says that he cannot or will not pay you the stated or known salary, ask him why, showing your astonishment. After he responds, and no matter what his response may be, ask what he is willing to pay you. If he quotes a starting salary that is even marginally acceptable, and you want the job, ask if he will agree to review your performance at the end of six months and then, if your performance has been up to his expectations, increase the salary to what you are worth and pay you the difference between that and the starting salary on a retroactive basis. Tell him you would be more than willing to take the job with the understanding that, if he is not satisfied with your performance at the end of the six month period, you will resign your position without argument. Assure him that you are willing to take that chance because you know that your performance will prove to be more than satisfactory. Faced with that proposition, he cannot avoid giving you a direct and meaningful answer.

If he does not accept your proposal, ask what he would suggest as an alternative. The important thing is to get the salary up to a satisfactory level within a reasonable length of time after you are hired.

*   *   *

If you have paid close attention while reading this chapter, you now know everything that is necessary to be effective and successful in the game of salary negotiation. For it *is* a game, as you can see; but it is a critical one, because until there has been a meeting of minds on the issue of compensation, you have not landed a job. The easy thing to do would be to accept the starting salary that the employer first offers, but in most cases you can do better than that. And remember, you will never lose a job offer by trying, *with tact*, to negotiate a higher salary.

When you have carried the salary negotiations as far as you can, with reasonableness and tact, and after you have received a firm job offer, you must then evaluate the total package that has been placed before you and decide whether to accept the position. Even if you already have concluded that you don't want the job on the terms negotiated, don't turn it down on the spot. Hold off as long as you can to see if other jobs materialize. In the meantime, thank the employer for his time and for the job offer. Tell him that you need some time to think about it and that you will get back to him in a couple of days. Be sure to call him with your decision within the time promised, and follow up your telephone call with an appropriate written response as discussed in Chapter 9.

When you accept a job offer, be sure to tell the employer that, in order to make certain that you have not misinterpreted any part of the agreement, you will send him a letter of acceptance (see Chapter 9) itemizing the terms of employment as you understand them. This will serve as a record of such terms for future reference. Don't antagonize him by asking him to "put it in writing". Do it yourself, as suggested here, but don't surprise him with it. Let him know in advance that you will be sending the letter.

> *"Question: Do you consider ten dollars a week enough for a longshoreman with a family to support?*
> *Answer: If that's all he can get, and he takes it, I should say it's enough."*
>
> —J. Pierpont Morgan

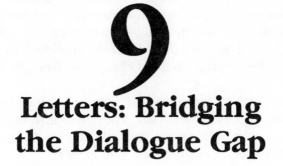

Letters: Bridging the Dialogue Gap

Letter writing is a vital and necessary part of the job-search campaign. It is essential to establishing and maintaining communications with the people you meet. Letters provide a continuity in the dialogue you initiate with those people, keeping them reminded of you and your potential value to them. They convey your appreciation for courtesies extended to you and, simultaneously, can be used to correct any misunderstandings or erroneous information that may have occurred during a prior interview or telephone conversation.

Before you have need to write your first letter, visit a print shop and order a supply of personalized stationery. Actually, this should be done during the earliest stages of planning your job-search campaign. It is not optional. Your letter is your personal emissary, and you want it to carry a subliminal message that you care about appearances and are attentive to detail. While the cost will vary from one geographical area to another, it will be nominal in comparison with the resulting enhancement to your image.

Choose a good quality stationery with a relatively high fiber content. Paper with a 25 percent cotton fiber content will be quite satisfactory. Anything with a lower fiber content should be avoided, while anything higher would call for needless extravagance. If saving a few dollars is important to you, a somewhat lesser quality, but not cheap, envelope will suffice.

Select plain white, buff or a very light gray paper for your letterhead, 8½ x 11 inches in size. The envelope should be the same color as the letter stock. It should be a No. 10 envelope, which measures approximately 4 x 10 inches.

The letterhead imprint should be of a conservative and formal block-style typeface, in black ink only. No script; nothing fancy. It should be centered at the top of the letter stock and should include your name, address and telephone number. Your name should be stated formally here. Nicknames definitely are out of order. The return address to be printed on the envelope (preferably on the sealing flap) will be identical to the letterhead imprint, minus the telephone number.

People at print shops usually have had a lot of experience in helping customers with their selection of paper, typeface, and colors of ink and with their sundry printing problems. Let them help you, too.

Basically, you will be concerned with eight different types of letters during the course of your campaign. They are:

1. The direct-approach letter.
2. The indirect-approach letter.
3. The referral follow-up letter.
4. The ad-response letter.
5. The letter of availability.
6. The thank-you letter.

7. The acceptance letter.
8. The wrap-up letter.

Each of these will be discussed in detail, with suggestions of when and how to use them and how to prepare them. Examples of the types of letters covered in this chapter appear in Appendix B in the back of this book. Use them as a guide to preparing similar letters in your own words, reflecting your own personality. But don't copy them. Otherwise, you will portray someone unlike yourself, and this could cause some awkward moments later. Not only that, but imagine the reaction of an employer receiving, from different individuals, identical letters copied from this book.

Now, let's discuss each type of letter in its turn.

THE DIRECT-APPROACH LETTER

The direct-approach letter is one in which the writer comes right out and asks for a job. It is the type of letter most commonly used in trying to make job contacts. Yet asking for a job is the least effective way of getting interviews, because it places employers in an awkward, uncomfortable position and immediately puts them on the defensive. For this reason, use of the direct-approach letter is not recommended and no further attention will be given to it here.

THE INDIRECT-APPROACH LETTER

The indirect-approach letter is used for the purpose of getting interviews with people in your business community under the pretense of seeking advice concerning your job search. The actual purpose, however, is to uncover hidden job opportunities. With this type of letter you are making a "cold" approach to someone with whom you have little or no connection and to whom you have not been referred by someone else. It is the key to obtaining referrals and expanding your network of job contacts. The basic intent of the letter is to prepare the recipient for a telephone call to set an appointment for an interview. It will enable you to get past his secretary, since you can truthfully tell her that her boss is expecting your call.

Business people, as a general rule, relate very closely to their communities. They usually try to discourage valuable or promising members of the community from moving away and, with the same interest at heart, do whatever they can to bring good people into the area. Therefore, by making a favorable impression with your letter, you are almost certain to be granted an interview, if for no other reason than to make sure that you are knowledgeable of the opportunities available in your own community.

In the first paragraph of your letter, you should let the reader know, by making some positive or even flattering statement about him, why you decided to write to him; but be careful that the words do not come across as being insincere and contrived.

Many people, in preparing this type of letter, make the mistake of elaborating upon their career accomplishments and objectives. You should avoid doing this. In fact, don't even mention your background and qualifications. Doing so could lead the recipient to the conclusion that you plan to ask him for a job and might put him on the defensive, in which case your letter may be forwarded routinely to the personnel department. So, give your assurance that you will not ask for a job and save all information concerning your background and qualifications for the interview.

See Appendix B for an example of how an indirect-approach letter should be written.

THE REFERRAL FOLLOW-UP LETTER

This form of letter is used to follow up a referral given to you at an advice interview.

Referrals usually should be followed up first by letter and then by telephone. Always send a letter before you attempt to make telephone contact if the person who gave you the referral:

- Refuses to call or write on your behalf to a referral he knows or who knows of him.
- Suggests the name of someone you should meet but does not know him or her personally.
Or,
- Suggests an organization that he thinks might be right for you, but is not acquainted with anyone affiliated with it.

The referral follow-up letter should be structured in the following manner:

1. State the name and company affiliation of the person who referred you, and mention that he or she suggested that you contact the individual to whom you are writing in order to seek his or her advice.
2. Mention your title and/or level of responsibility and identify your organizational affiliation, either by name or by reference to its industrial classification (chemical, steel, utility industry, etc.).
3. Briefly describe your present state of affairs and what you are doing about it; for example:

   "Although I have been well satisfied with my career progress thus far, I foresee very little opportunity for advancement from my present position. It is time, I believe, to make a change, and I have initiated a well planned job-search campaign to do just that."
4. Emphasize your assurance that you do not expect to be offered a job and that you will not ask for one, in a manner similar to the following:

   "I want to make it clear that I do not expect you to have, or to know of, a job which would be right for me at this time, and I assure you that I do not intend to bring that subject up. However, at Mr. _____'s suggestion, I would like to meet with you to get your thoughts and advice concerning my approach to my job search."

5. Establish a specific date and time for your follow-up telephone call to arrange a meeting. This will enable you to tell whoever answers the telephone that your call is expected. More important, it allows you to stay in control of the situation by leaving the arrangement of a meeting to your own initiative. Otherwise, you may never get a response to your letter. The date specified for the follow-up call should be about a week after the mailing of the letter.

THE AD-RESPONSE LETTER

Preparation of the ad-response letter, used to answer classified job-advertisements, is covered in Chapter 3. A sample letter appears in Appendix B.

THE LETTER OF AVAILABILITY

The letter of availability simply announces that you are looking for a job and requests an interview. You should send as many of these letters as there are companies which interest you, because the more letters you send, the greater the probability that you will uncover a job opportunity.

However, there are only two situations in which the letter of availability should be used:

1. Where an indirect "cold-approach" or a referral follow-up has been unsuccessful in getting an advice interview.
2. Where a company you are interested in contacting is beyond reasonable one-day, round-trip driving distance.

When your efforts to get an advice interview have proved fruitless, you may as well make the most of the situation by sending a letter of availability. When you originally contacted the individual to request a meeting for advice, you promised that you would not ask for a job at the interview. By sending him a letter of availability, you will not be reneging on that promise, because (1) the interview failed to materialize, and (2) your intention is only to make it clear that you are *available* for hiring. Under these conditions, you should not follow up the letter with a telephone call as in other instances. That would be tantamount to asking for a job and, under the circumstances, would be overly aggressive. Don't make any further effort to contact this person unless you receive a response to your letter of availability. If the response is positive, then you should call to arrange a job interview. If it is negative, try again for an advice interview. If you get no response at all, forget it.

In your letter of availability to a distantly located company, however, you should make it clear that you are hoping a job opportunity might be available there. In that letter, therefore, you should indicate that, unless you get a response, you will call to find out whether or not your letter has prompted any interest.

Notice that the two sample letters of availability shown in Appendix B are quite similar in structure and, although slanted somewhat differently, carry basically the same message. Also note that, despite my earlier admonishment to be stingy and selective in handing out your resume, a functional resume (not a chronological one — too much detail; too dry) should accompany the letter of availability, because you want to tell the reader enough about your capabilities to make him or her want to know more; and this is the only way you can do that in these circumstances.

THE THANK-YOU LETTER

Thank-you letters, in addition to showing ordinary courtesy, play a major role in a job-search campaign. Don't ever fail to send a thank-you letter each time someone has helped you, or even tried to help you, in any way. People like to feel that favors they do for others are appreciated, and it is natural for them to become indifferent to those who do not properly acknowledge their help. Don't take the chance of alienating a valuable ally by failing to write a brief, simple letter of thanks. Be prompt in sending your thank-you letters, and take great care and show sincerity as you write them.

The occasions during your job campaign which will require thank-you letters are:

1. After you have had an advice interview, regardless of whether or not you consider it to have been beneficial to you.
2. Following a job interview. In this instance, the general tone of the letter will depend upon the outcome of the interview; that is, (a) whether there clearly is continued interest in you as a candidate for the position, (b) whether you were definitely turned down for the job or (c) whether you decide to reject a job offer made during the interview.

Your letter of thanks following an advice interview should be simple and brief. You need only to extend your appreciation for the time made available to you and for the help and suggestions you received. And even if you feel you got nothing of value from the interview, don't let that attitude show in your letter.

When you have had a job interview and a definite interest in your qualifications has been clearly indicated, along with an expressed intention to be in touch with you later, the thank-you letter gives you an opportunity to clarify matters discussed at the interview, if need be, as well as to introduce additional information.

The letter should be structured to include the following:

1. Obviously, you should express your apprecia-

tion for the interview.

2. If, during the interview, you discovered something in which the employer has a special
interest, or that the two of you have very much
in common, mention it in the letter. This will
serve to enhance your rapport with him or her.

3. Bring up any important information that you
may have omitted during the interview.

4. Clarify or correct anything that you feel may
have been misunderstood.

5. Specify when you will call the employer to
determine what his or her thoughts are at that
time concerning you and the job.

If you are turned down for a job, either during or following an
interview, you should maintain your courtesy by sending the
employer a brief letter of thanks for the time he made available
to you. Point out that he now knows a lot about your
background and qualifications and ask if, with this in mind, he
could suggest anyone else in his company — or outside of it, for
that matter — with whom you should meet. In any event, keep
the situation under your control by telling him you will call in a
few days to see if he, in fact, has thought of any such
suggestions. If he feels at all remorseful about having to turn
you down for the job, he may refer you to someone else.

There may be a time when you will judge it in your best interest
to turn down a job offer. The chances of this occurring are
minimal, but it could happen. If it does, it is nonetheless
advisable to follow through with a letter of thanks to the
employer. Make it brief. Tell him why you have decided against
accepting the job. It may be that the finally negotiated salary is
lower than you can accept or that your future prospects in the
company do not appear to be as promising as you would like
them to be, but be tactful with whatever you say. Ask him if, in
view of what he has learned about your qualifications and
background of experience, he knows of anyone else you might
talk to. After having turned down his job offer it is unlikely that

he will want to help you, but, then again, he may. Anyway, you
have nothing to lose by trying. Finally, tell him that you will be
in contact with him in a few days to see if he has any suggestions
in that regard.

In Chapter 8, you were cautioned never to reject a job offer on
the spot. That advice deserves reemphasis here. Always allow
yourself time to thoroughly consider a job offer before turning
it down.

THE ACCEPTANCE LETTER

When you have accepted a job offer, you should confirm it by
sending a letter of acceptance to the employer. It also makes
good sense to have a written record of the terms of employment
that have been agreed to, and the acceptance letter is a logical
medium for acomplishing this. It is far better for you to get the
employment terms on record in this manner than to offend the
employer by asking him to "put it in writing". However, when
you accept the job offer, be sure to tell the employer that, in
order to be certain that you have not misconstrued any of the
things that have been agreed upon, you will be sending him a
letter outlining the terms of employment as you understand
them. Don't let it come as a surprise to him. You don't want to
start out by antagonizing your new employer.

The acceptance letter should be prepared in the following
format:

> *First paragraph* — With an air of enthusiasm and
> gratitude, confirm your acceptance of the job
> offer, making sure to mention the title of the
> position.
> *Second paragraph* — Reaffirm your understanding
> of the major responsibilities of the position and its
> reporting level.
> *Third paragraph* — Confirm the base salary, fringe
> benefits and any other compensation agreed
> upon, including moving and temporary living

expenses, use of a company car, club memberships, etc.

Fourth paragraph — Confirm any promises for the future that accompanied the job offer.

Fifth paragraph — Mention the date when you are to report to work, followed by an appropriate closing statement.

THE WRAP-UP LETTER

When your job-search campaign finally comes to an end, and you have a job definitely in hand, you should turn your attention back to those who helped you along the way: the friends, relatives and acquaintances who gave you continuing encouragement; the many people who took time from their busy schedules to give you advice; and those who helped you to meet others. Wrap up your campaign by reviewing your files and sending each of these individuals a letter telling them about your new job and the organization you are now affiliated with, thanking them for the help they gave you and offering your help if they or any of their friends or associates should ever need similar assistance. These letters should go out within two or three weeks after you have concluded your search. Do not, by any means, allow this final phase of your program to slip by, because to do so would be an inexcusable breach of etiquette. And, although it may not seem likely to you now, you may need help again from these people some day.

> *"Be obscure clearly."*
>
> —E.B. White

10

It's Over — Now What?

Congratulations! You have landed a job. Not only that, but because you followed the principles discussed in this book, your new position is, in all likelihood, close to or better than what you had hoped for in the way of salary and responsibilities. In fact, you probably are one of the relatively few, of all the many people looking for jobs, who was able to complete a job search with such success. Now you want your success to continue. You want not only to be able to hold on to the job you have worked so hard to get, but also to reap the greater rewards that come with steady advancement to higher positions. This means that, in addition to being extremely capable in carrying out your duties and responsibilities, you must stand out from the crowd. In this chapter, you will learn how to protect yourself in your new job and how to gain acceptance and special recognition by the upper echelons of the organization.

By the time you are hired for a job, your capabilities are taken for granted. This is especially true if you are in one of the higher-level positions. The employer spent a lot of time interviewing you and asked a lot of pointed questions in an effort to evaluate your abilities, and he would not have hired you had he not been thoroughly convinced that you have all it takes, and more, to handle the job. That being the case, it is especially important to focus your efforts toward the one other area that is vital to your ability to hold on to your job and to advance in the organization: the ubiquitous practice of office politics. For many, the very mention of office politics raises negative reactions, even disgust and contempt. Nevertheless, it is unavoidably present in every organization, and, if you are to survive, much less prosper, you must be willing and able to deal with it. The lengths you will follow in dealing with it will depend upon how important it is to you to protect yourself in your job and how ambitious you are for advancement. To some, it is a loathsome pursuit; to others, it is an exciting, Machiavellian game. You must make your own decision as to the extent of your involvement in this sometimes risky contest. Fortunately, there are ways to participate in office politics that will enable you to keep your self-respect and, at the same time, insulate you from the risk of alienating others in the process.

Remember this: although you hold your position, with its accompanying authority and power, at the discretion of higher management, the effectiveness of your authority depends ultimately upon the willingness of your subordinates to yield to it. If they want to, they can have you out of your job in a very short time. All that is required is an insidious perpetration of failure on their part to cooperate with you on some matter of substantial importance to the company, and you will never know what happened or why. It is obvious, then, that although you must be tough-minded and firm in dealing with your subordinates, it always is in your best interest to treat them with courtesy and respect. And never reprimand or criticize anyone in the presence of others. If it is necessary to take someone to task, do it in privacy. There is no useful purpose to be served by degrading another human being, and the topic of your displeasure is no one else's business.

Beware of becoming socially involved or building friendships with your subordinates. Usually, the only interest that you have in common with them is your affiliation with the same company, and, invariably, your conversations at cocktail parties or on the golf course will turn to and dwell on company related topics. In a relaxed atmosphere, especially after imbibing, the conversation often drifts into areas of confidentiality, leading to comments that would better be left unspoken. And how do you handle a situation where you have no alternative but to demote or fire someone with whom you frequently have partied or who has been your golf buddy? Awkwardly, that's how! So it is best for you, and for the people working for you, to keep your relationships on a business level. This also applies where your peers are concerned, because one of you could become the other's boss someday, again making for an awkward and uncomfortable situation. So, if a subordinate employee or one of your peers makes social overtures to you, politely refuse with a plausible excuse. After a few unsuccessful efforts he will get the message, without embarrassment, if you choose your words with care.

No matter how good you are at your job, or whose "fair-haired boy" you are, there always may be someone who wants you out. If so, it could be someone you have the least reason to suspect, someone who gives every appearance of being "in your corner". On the other hand, your enemy may make no secret of his or her opposition to you. This person obviously either looks upon you as a threat to his or her position and future prospects in the company or merely has taken a strong dislike to you. Who might this be, then? Well, unfortunately, it could be almost anyone. It could be your boss, if he feels insecure in his position and, therefore, threatened by you. It could be a close subordinate who is so eager to have your job that he goes out of his way to drop poisoned remarks about you to your boss and to others in management. Or it could be one of your peers who views you as a deterrent to his own advancement in the company and is attempting to prejudice the opinions of others, especially your superiors, against you. So, from the very beginning in your new job, it is important to build good relationships at all levels and to take other steps that will protect you in the event that you may someday find yourself in this precarious situation.

Keep a notebook in your desk for the sole purpose of making notes concerning any significant accomplishments in your job. Make a record in it of each major task or project assigned to you, including a brief description of it, dates it was started and completed, problems encountered and how they were handled, final results or conclusions and a quantification of expected and realized benefits to the company. With these notes at hand, you will be prepared to document your achievements if ever your capabilities are questioned. They also will serve as a booster during regular performance reviews.

It has been said that a person who never makes mistakes or experiences failure is one who never does anything. Therefore, it is unlikely that fortune will be so kind as to allow you to be free from error or fault in everything you do. One measure of a person's character is his or her propensity to accept responsibility for his own mistakes or failures. So, if you err in judgement or fact, or if you fail at something you undertake to do, accept the blame. Don't try to pass it on to someone else. And don't make excuses. Reasons, good or poor, are acceptable; excuses are not. Chances are that, by standing up to your mistakes and failures this way (and providing they don't happen often), you will gain respect and admiration.

When you interview for a job, you stress again and again your many strengths and capabilities, and, as mentioned before, by the time a job offer is made, these are taken for granted. This is particularly true for positions at professional and department head levels or higher. Therefore, no matter what your job is and provided you did not exaggerate your claims, your future with the company depends almost entirely upon getting along well with others and being recognized as a team player.

Here are some suggestions to help you to ingratiate yourself with the people who count (and, believe me, everyone counts) and to establish yourself as a team player:

- Although you must be firm and show self-confidence in your dealings with people, always be fair and courteous to everyone; and be honest — with yourself as well as with others.

- Keep a good sense of humor and let a trace of it show through in your personality — when appropriate, of course.

- Cultivate a good relationship with your boss and with others in higher management.

- Look for centers of influence — the power centers — in the organization and align yourself with them. Take your time with this. Don't be overly aggressive, and avoid any appearance of being an apple polisher.

- If you are invited to lunch, go. But if drinks are offered, casually order something non-alcoholic. At company social gatherings, feel free to have a drink if others do and if it pleases you, but be moderate. Excessive drinking loosens one's inhibitions and leads to careless and indiscreet conduct.

- Be on the lookout for ways to increase your contribution to the company. Do everything you can to be regarded as a team player. You can add credibility to this role by volunteering to take on additional duties or responsibilities, even though they may not be directly related to your job. This could be in the form of an offer to help others who are overloaded with work. But be careful not to give the impression that you are trying to take over someone else's job.

- Never complain about your job, your boss or company policies. Complaints often are exaggerated and distorted and tend to find their way to ears not intended to hear them.

- Don't argue with your boss or fight him. Whenever there is a difference of opinion, state your case and be sure he understands it. Then, do as he says without further comment. On the other hand, don't be a yes man, who is of no real value to anyone.

- Make your boss look good. A promotion for him could mean one for you, as well.

- Finally, be sure to recognize that, for the most part, the actions of all living beings — including humans — are motivated, more or less, by two basic emotions: fear and greed. If you can accept this and abide by it, you will be in a far better position to influence others to your own best advantage.

*　　　*　　　*

Most people are average in most ways. My purpose in writing this book has been to help you to become a great deal better than average — a winner, in fact — in the job market and in your work environment. I have an unshakable belief that you can do anything or be anything you wish, provided you have a burning desire for it and that you are willing to dedicate not only your time and effort, but your whole being, to achieving it. Therefore, turn back and reread this book — not once, but again and again. Read it until it becomes a part of you, and, even then, refer to it from time to time as a refresher.

You can have the job and the success of your dreams. All you have to do is work for them. But first, you have to know what to do and how to do it. I think you are ready now.

Good Luck!

Appendix A
Sample Resumes

Chronological Resume

JOHN J. SEARCHER

1223 Westcott Avenue
Harbison, Michigan 35204
(617) 863-6529

OBJECTIVE: Senior financial management position

EXPERIENCE: MIDWEST STEEL COMPANY
<u>Vice President - Finance and Accounting</u>
<u>Responsibilities</u>: All accounting, tax,
financial planning and treasury functions,
including timely availability of cash funds.
Also, corporate computer services and
internal auditing. Planning and execution of
issuance of all types of securities. Heavy
customer relations responsibilities.

<u>Results</u>: Maintained relative financial
strength of company in face of industry
decline. Recommended and directed
installation and implementation of a
computerized customer information system,
with annual savings of $500,000 to
$700,000.

Controller
<u>Responsibilities</u>: All accounting, tax,
budgeting and computer functions.
Management representative on union
contract negotiating team. Heavy customer
relations responsibilities.

<u>Results</u>: Effectively managed all controller-
ship functions. Administered a very
complex joint-venture contract with a major
oil company. Acted as liaison and principal
negotiator for the company and, as such,
held the line on many issues involving cost
sharing resulting in substantial savings
(increased profits).

Chronological Resume (cont'd.)

— 2 —

Assistant Controller
Responsibilities: All accounting and budgeting functions. Substantial customer relations responsibilities.

Results: Integrated stores accounting and physical inventory records, merging two separate clerical forces into one group. This resulted in significant reduction in personnel.

Manager, General Accounting Department
Responsibilities: All general accounting functions, including consolidation accounting, budgeting, and financial and statistical reporting (both internal and external).

Results: Researched, recommended and directed the conversion of a manual payroll accounting system to a fully computerized one.

Accountant
Responsibilities: General accounting functions, including consolidation accounting and performance of special accounting studies.

Results: Designed and implemented an accounting system to meet the requirements of a very complex joint-venture contract with a major oil company.

BEAKER CHEMICAL COMPANY
Cost Accountant

SERVE-ALL UTILITIES
Accountant

Chronological Resume (cont'd.)

— 3 —

EDUCATION:	B.B.A., Southwest University
	M.B.A., Worthington College
	Executive development courses: Rutgers University, University of Richmond, and American Management Association.
MILITARY EXPERIENCE:	U.S. Army
PERSONAL:	Health excellent; happily married with three wonderful children.
MEMBERSHIPS:	Rotary International
	Kiwanis International
	Michigan State Chamber of Commerce
	National Association of Accountants
OTHER ACTIVITIES:	Surf fishing
	Tennis
	Music and reading

Functional Resume

JOHN J. SEARCHER

1223 Westcott Avenue
Harbison, Michigan 35204
(617) 863-6529

OBJECTIVE: Senior financial management position.

QUALIFICATIONS: Successively increasing financial responsibilities and achievements in a large nationally-known electric and gas utility company, an internationally-known chemical manufacturer and a major steel-producing company.

Positions held:
- Vice President - Finance and Accounting
- Controller
- Assistant Controller
- Manager-General Accounting
- Accountant

SOME FUNCTIONAL BACKGROUND EXAMPLES

TOP-LEVEL
PLANNING   Advised the Board of Directors to adopt a new dividend policy designed to increase the market value of the common stock of the company to a level in excess of book value. The dividend was increased as recommended and the market value of the stock improved as expected.

Established and followed a corporate financial policy which substantially strengthened the capital structure of the company. This was accomplished by exercising precision and skill in determining the timing and types of new securities sales.

Functional Resume (cont'd.)

— 2 —

CREATIVITY | Planned and directed the installation and implementation of a computerized responsibility accounting system, a computerized maintenance work order system and a very sophisticated customer information system at a total cost of $6,000,000, resulting in savings of $700,000 to $950,000 annually.

Developed a special method of accounting for a contract-termination settlement amounting to $225 million in favor of the company and formulated strategy which minimized related income tax consequences. These were recognized as innovations since the transaction was unprecedented in the industry.

FORESIGHT/ INITIATIVE | Recommended and directed the planning and implementation of a computerized management information system which increased efficiencies in all departments, providing more timely, sophisticated information to management.

Recommended and implemented an intensive investor relations program, resulting in improvement in the credit rating of the company's senior securities and increased attraction of investors to all securities of the company.

PERSUASIVENESS | Obtained the "swing" votes necessary to achieve a very critical amendment to the Articles of Incorporation of the company, involving a matter of severe financial implications. Personal

Functional Resume (cont'd.)

— 3 —

attention to a small group of influential shareholders made this achievement possible.

Convinced the major securities rating agencies to maintain the satisfactory rating of the company's securities at a time when credit ratings of other companies in the industry were rapidly deteriorating. This was accomplished by establishing exceptional rapport with rating agency personnel and developing a reputation for extreme credibility.

**EMPLOYMENT
HISTORY:**

MIDWEST STEEL COMPANY
Vice-President — Finance and
   Accounting
Controller
Assistant Controller
Manager-General Accounting
Accountant

BEAKER CHEMICAL COMPANY
Cost Accountant

SERVE-ALL UTILITIES
Accountant

EDUCATION:

B.B.A., Southwest University
M.B.A., Worthington College
Various recognized executive
development programs.

**MILITARY
EXPERIENCE:**

U.S. Army

PERSONAL:

Health excellent; happily married with
three wonderful children.

Functional Resume (cont'd.)

— 4 —

MEMBERSHIPS: Rotary International
Kiwanis International
Michigan State Chamber of Commerce
National Association of Accountants

OTHER
  ACTIVITIES: Surf fishing
Tennis
Music and reading

Appendix B
Sample Letters

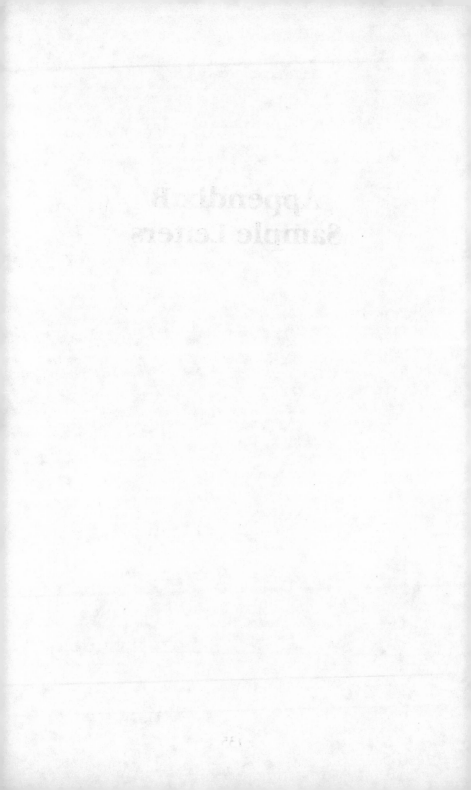

Indirect-approach Letter

Robert Brown
2311 Eastlake Drive
Rockford, Illinois 61108

September 17, 19__

Daniel Rogers, President
Chemical Compounds, Inc.
805 Industrial Circle
Rockford, Illinois 61108

Dear Mr. Rogers:

One way to get new career exposure is through the often used
"request for advice", of which you probably have received many.
However, I am sure that you, as a highly placed executive, are
always sensitive to the importance of the recognition and demonstra-
tion of individual values, even outside of your own organization;
and since I am facing a career change, I am hopeful that an exchange
of ideas might be mutually beneficial.

I am Director of Finance for a well known multi-million dollar
Midwestern chemical company, having advanced to that position by way
of successively increasing responsibilities in accounting and
financial management. A restructuring of our organization has placed
me in the unenviable position of facing a reduction in my responsibilities, and I have too many years of effective contribution to make
to accept such a diminished role. Therefore, I feel that it is time
for me to move on, and I have initiated a job-search campaign to do
just that.

Since this is the first real job campaign of my life, I need some
objective advice from top executives like you, both within and outside of my field, and I believe you can help me. One thing I would
like to discuss with you is the question of possible relocation,
which naturally arises whenever one considers a change of employment.

Toward that end, I will call you on Wednesday of next week, in the
afternoon, to see if we can arrange a brief meeting. If you can
spare a few minutes of your time, I would be most grateful; if you
cannot, I will understand. In either event, I do not expect you to
have, or to know of, a job which would be right for me at this time,
and I assure you that I do not intend to ask for one. I am looking
only for direction.

Many thanks for your interest and understanding.

Sincerely yours,

Referral Follow-up Letter

Robert Brown
2311 Eastlake Drive
Rockford, Illinois 61108

September 17, 19___

Daniel Rogers, President
Chemical Compounds, Inc.
805 Industrial Circle
Rockford, Illinois 61108

Dear Mr. Rogers:

I was talking to Mr. Richard Johnson of the Apex Steel Company a
few days ago, and he suggested that I write to you since you are so
greatly attuned to the business community in this area.

I am in the process of making some very important decisions
concerning a possible change of employment and I am in need of
advice. I believe you can help me. Let me assure you that I have
no expectations of your having a job for me, nor do I intend to ask
you for one. I want only your advice.

Whenever a change of employment is considered, the question of
relocating naturally arises, but I prefer not to do so unless I have
to. I would like to talk to a few people, such as yourself, about
the advisability of remaining in this area and to discuss, and hear
opinions of, the opportunities that might be available here, now or
in the future, for someone with my qualifications.

I would be grateful if you would be so kind as to allow me about
half an hour of your valuable time. In the hope that you will be
able to accomodate me, I will call you on Wednesday of next week,
in the afternoon, to see if we can arrange a meeting at a time
suitable to you.

Sincerely yours,

Robert Brown

Ad-response Letter

Robert Brown
2311 Eastlake Drive
Rockford, Illinois 61108

September 17, 19__

David Marks, Vice President
Alpha Chemical Company
1015 Kentwood Avenue
Baltimore, Maryland 21210

Dear Mr. Marks:

This is in response to your advertisement in The Wall Street Ju
on September 15, 19__, for a Director of Finance.

Since I have not been actively looking for work, I have no current
resume. Therefore, I have listed below the indicated requirements of
the position and my qualifications as they relate to them:

Requirements	Qualifications
1. Familiarity with current accounting principles.	1. My present position requires that I keep currently abreast of all pronouncements of the American Institute of Certified Public Accountants.
2. Knowledge of budgeting and forecasting.	2. I am presently responsible for the preparation and monitoring of all budgets and forecasts for my company.
3. Knowledge of SEC rules and regulations.	3. One of my current responsibilities is the preparation and filing of all reports and applications to the Securities and Exchange Commission.
4. Supervisory experience.	4. I have had managerial responsibilities in the areas of finance and accounting for the past six years.

I would like an opportunity to elaborate on my background and experience
in person and will call you to arrange a meeting for this purpose at
your convenience. [Or, if it is a blind ad, "...and am looking forward
to hearing from you to arrange a meeting for this purpose."]

Sincerely yours,

Robert Brown

Letter of Availability to a Distantly Located Company

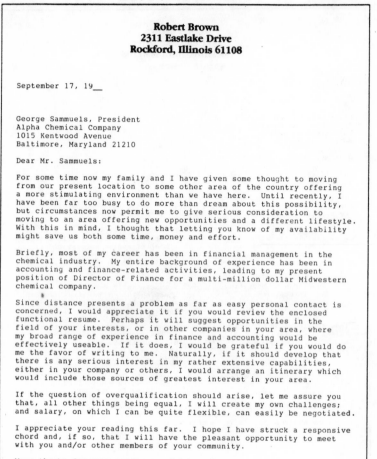

Robert Brown
2311 Eastlake Drive
Rockford, Illinois 61108

September 17, 19__

George Sammuels, President
Alpha Chemical Company
1015 Kentwood Avenue
Baltimore, Maryland 21210

Dear Mr. Sammuels:

For some time now my family and I have given some thought to moving
from our present location to some other area of the country offering
a more stimulating environment than we have here. Until recently, I
have been far too busy to do more than dream about this possibility,
but circumstances now permit me to give serious consideration to
moving to an area offering new opportunities and a different lifestyle.
With this in mind, I thought that letting you know of my availability
might save us both some time, money and effort.

Briefly, most of my career has been in financial management in the
chemical industry. My entire background of experience has been in
accounting and finance-related activities, leading to my present
position of Director of Finance for a multi-million dollar Midwestern
chemical company.

Since distance presents a problem as far as easy personal contact is
concerned, I would appreciate it if you would review the enclosed
functional resume. Perhaps it will suggest opportunities in the
field of your interests, or in other companies in your area, where
my broad range of experience in finance and accounting would be
effectively useable. If it does, I would be grateful if you would do
me the favor of writing to me. Naturally, if it should develop that
there is any serious interest in my rather extensive capabilities,
either in your company or others, I would arrange an itinerary which
would include those sources of greatest interest in your area.

If the question of overqualification should arise, let me assure you
that, all other things being equal, I will create my own challenges;
and salary, on which I can be quite flexible, can easily be negotiated.

I appreciate your reading this far. I hope I have struck a responsive
chord and, if so, that I will have the pleasant opportunity to meet
with you and/or other members of your community.

Many thanks for your courtesy and interest.

Sincerely yours,

Robert Brown

Letter of Availability Following an Unsuccessful Request for an Advice Interview

Robert Brown
2311 Eastlake Drive
Rockford, Illinois 61108

September 17, 19__

Daniel Rogers, President
Chemical Compounds, Inc.
805 Industrial Circle
Rockford, Illinois 61108

Dear Mr. Rogers:

I wrote to you a few weeks ago in the hope that I could meet with you
to get your advice concerning my decision to make a career change;
but, unfortunately, we were unable to arrange such a meeting, and I
fully understand.

I am writing to you now to remind you of my availability. I would
appreciate it if you would review the enclosed functional resume in
the hope that it might suggest opportunities in the field of your
interests, or in other companies that you know of, where my extensive
financial expertise could be effectively utilized and that you would
do me the favor of writing to me or calling if this should be the
case. Relocation, if necessary, would present no problem.

To expand briefly on my background, most of my career has been in
financial management and control in the chemical industry. My entire
experience has been in accounting and budgetary activities, leading to
my present position of Director of Finance of a large Midwestern
chemical company.

If there should be a question of overqualification, let me assure you
that I would create my own challenges; and compensation, on which I
can be quite flexible, is less important to me than a stimulating job
environment and prospects for the future.

Thank you for reading this far. I hope I have struck a responsive
chord and, if so, that I will be hearing from you and/or from other
companies that may come to your mind.

Many thanks for your courtesy and interest.

Sincerely yours,

Robert Brown

Thank-you Letter Following an Advice Interview

Robert Brown
2311 Eastlake Drive
Rockford, Illinois 61108

September 17, 19__

Daniel Rogers, President
Chemical Compounds, Inc.
805 Industrial Circle
Rockford, Illinois 61108

Dear Mr. Rogers:

I want to thank you again for giving me so much of your time last
Tuesday and for the valuable advice and suggestions I received.

I have already written to Mr. Warren about arranging an interview.
If you think of anyone else I should talk to I would appreciate
hearing from you.

If you don't mind, I will take the liberty of advising you from
time to time of my progress.

Sincerely yours,

Robert Brown

Thank-you Letter Following a Job Interview —
Candidate Rejects Job Offer

Robert Brown
2311 Eastlake Drive
Rockford, Illinois 61108

September 17, 19__

David Marks, Vice President
Alpha Chemical Company
1015 Kentwood Avenue
Baltimore, Maryland 21210

Dear Mr. Marks:

Thank you for the time you made available to me last Thursday and for
the offer of the position of Director of Finance with your company.
Regretfully, I feel that it would not be in my best long-range interest
to accept the position. I have no doubts concerning my qualifications
for the job and am extremely confident of my ability to make a
substantial contribution toward meeting your corporate objectives.
However, any advancement opportunity appears to be so far into the
future as to severely limit the full utilization of my capabilities.

In view of what you have learned about my background and experience,
perhaps you know of someone else I should talk to. I will call you
in a few days to see if you have any suggestions in that regard.

Sincerely yours,

Robert Brown

Thank-you Letter Following a Job Interview —
Continued Interest in Candidate

Robert Brown
2311 Eastlake Drive
Rockford, Illinois 61108

September 17, 19__

George Sammuels, President
Alpha Chemical Company
1015 Kentwood Avenue
Baltimore, Maryland 21210

Dear Mr. Sammuels:

I want to thank you for being so generous with your time at our
meeting last Thursday. Although far off from the main subject, I must
say I was delighted to learn of your special interest in music; and
our discussion of Mozart was an unexpected treat.

I would like to take this opportunity to mention something which I
inadvertantly omitted during our interview, and I think it is important. During 19__, I was on loan to the state of Illinois, on a part-
time basis, to serve on a committee to make recommendations to improve
the budgetary procedures of all departments of the state government.
Through this experience, I gained an insight into the workings of
state agencies and got a lot of ideas that proved beneficial to my
already considerable expertise in budgeting and forecasting.

I am concerned that I may not have clearly described the recent
developments affecting my present position. My job has not been
eliminated, but, due to the reorganization that has just taken place,
my responsibilities have been diluted to the extent that I no longer
have the challenges that I thrive on so much. We are trying to work
something out to improve the situation, but I cannot foresee a
satisfactory solution to the problem.

I am excited about the job at your company that we discussed, and I
will call you on Tuesday, September 25, in the afternoon, to find
out what your thoughts are at that time.

Sincerely yours,

Robert Brown

Thank-you Letter Following a Job Interview —
Candidate Turned Down for Job

Robert Brown
2311 Eastlake Drive
Rockford, Illinois 61108

September 17, 19__

David Marks, Vice President
Alpha Chemical Company
1015 Kentwood Avenue
Baltimore, Maryland 21210

Dear Mr. Marks:

I very much appreciate the time you made available to me yesterday
to discuss the position of Director of Finance for your company.
Although I still feel well qualified for the job, I clearly
understand the reasons for your decision to look to other candidates
to fill the position.

You have learned a great deal about my qualifications and background
of experience. With this in mind, can you suggest anyone else within
or outside of your company whom I should talk to? I will call you
in a few days to see if you have any thoughts in this regard.

Sincerely yours,

Robert Brown

The Acceptance Letter

Robert Brown
2311 Eastlake Drive
Rockford, Illinois 61108

September 17, 19___

David Marks, Vice President
Alpha Chemical Company
1015 Kentwood Avenue
Baltimore, Maryland 21210

Dear Mr. Marks:

I am delighted to accept the position of Director of Finance with
your company and am looking forward to the many challenges that await
me.

As I understand it, I will report directly to the Vice President of
Finance and will be primarily responsible for all accounting functions
budgeting and forecasting, tax management and all financial reporting.

We agreed upon a starting salary of $65,000 a year. The company will
provide, at its expense, contributions to a retirement plan; group
life insurance in accordance with company policy; hospitalization and
major medical insurance for me and, within stated limitations of the
plan, my immediate family; and memberships in the University Club and
one service club, such as Rotary, Kiwanis, etc. In addition, I will be
assigned an automobile to be used in accordance with company policy;
and the company will pay all moving expenses, excluding those related
to the purchase or sale of property, but including an allowance of up
to $900 a month for a period of three months for temporary living
quarters, if required.

It is my understanding that my performance will be reviewed at the
end of six months and that this will be followed by an increase in
salary as determined from the results of that review.

As previously agreed, I will report ready to work on Tuesday, October
1. I am anxious to get started.

Sincerely yours,

The Wrap-up Letter

Robert Brown
2311 Eastlake Drive
Rockford, Illinois 61108

October 15, 19__

Daniel Rogers, President
Chemical Compounds, Inc.
805 Industrial Circle
Rockford, Illinois 61108

Dear Mr. Rogers:

You were kind enough to meet with me several months ago to help me with some decision-making concerning my job-search campaign. I am very grateful for the help you gave me, and I think it will please you to know that my campaign has come to a successful end.

I am happy to report that next month I will assume the position of Director of Finance for the Alpha Chemical Company in Baltimore, Maryland. Although I regret having to leave this area, I am looking forward to the challenges of my new job and the different lifestyle afforded by an East Coast metropolitan area.

If ever there is anything I can do for you, or any of your friends or associates, please be sure to let me know.

Sincerely yours,

Robert Brown

Index

ORDER FORM

Dunmore Publishing Company
Dept. 1A, P.O. Box 2411
New Bern, NC 28561-2411
Telephone: (919) 636-1043

Please send me _____ copy(ies) of "Unlocking the Job Market" by James L. Hammond @ $16.95 each.

Shipping & handling: $2.00 for one book and $1.00 for each additional book.

North Carolina residents only: Please add sales tax of 85¢ per book.

No. of books ordered _____ Total amount of purchase $ _____

☐ Check   ☐ Money order   ☐ MasterCard   ☐ Visa

Card No. _____ Exp. date _____

Name _____ Tel. No. (   ) _____

Street & No. _____ Apt. No. _____

City _____ State _____ Zip _____

ORDER FORM

Dunmore Publishing Company
Dept. 1A, P.O. Box 2411
New Bern, NC 28561-2411
Telephone: (919) 636-1043

Please send me _____ copy(ies) of "Unlocking the Job Market" by James L. Hammond @ $16.95 each.

Shipping & handling: $2.00 for one book and $1.00 for each additional book.

North Carolina residents only: Please add sales tax of 85¢ per book.

No. of books ordered _____ Total amount of purchase $ _____

☐ Check   ☐ Money order   ☐ MasterCard   ☐ Visa

Card No. _____ Exp. date _____

Name _____ Tel. No. ( ) _____

Street & No. _____ Apt. No. _____

City _____ State _____ Zip _____